Morning
MANNA
FOR YOUR DAY

ONE-YEAR DEVOTIONAL

BY BISHOP GEOFFREY V. DUDLEY, SR., D.Min.

Morning Manna for Your Day—One-Year Devotional
by Bishop Geoffrey V. Dudley, Sr., D.Min.

The Church Online, LLC
1000 Ardmore Blvd.
Pittsburgh, PA 15221

International Standard Book Number: 978-1-940786-60-5

Library of Congress Catalogue Card Number: Available Upon Request

Printed in the United States of America

Published by The Church Online, LLC

DEDICATION

This book is dedicated to my loving parents, the late Bishop Leamon Dudley, Sr. and the late Mrs. Ida Dorothy Dudley. They instilled in me drive and devotion to God at an early age. It is because of their selfless love for God, my mother's persistent prayers, and my father's example as a pastor that I am where I am today.

ACKNOWLEDGEMENTS

I would like to thank my loyal and tenacious executive assistant, Dagne. Her "get it done" approach to everything enables me precious time to write. Additionally, I would like to thank Anne, who has been invaluable in the editing process.

Most of all, I want to thank my lovely wife, Glenda Dudley, of 35 plus years, and my amazing children Mahogany and Geoffrey II. You guys give me life and keep me young!

Table of Contents

INTRODUCTION

God is taking you on a journey. Every day is another gift from Him that takes you a step closer to your destiny.

But you need food to fuel you on your journey. When God led the Hebrew people out of slavery in Egypt to freedom in the promised land, He sustained them along the way with food from heaven—manna. Every morning the people awoke to find the ground covered with the sweet-tasting heavenly bread, and they went out to collect enough for that day. In God's miraculous provision, He made sure every man, woman, and child had exactly the amount of manna they needed. Nothing was left over and nothing went to waste.

God still provides food for your journey. But like the Hebrew people, you have to go out and collect it. *Morning Manna for Your Day* is a tool to guide you into God's presence so you can get the spiritual nourishment you need. Each day's devotion has three parts: The Text, The Talk, and The Takeaway. You'll find five devotions for each week along with a brief Weekend Reflection that will help you explore what God is doing in your life. Use the provided journaling space to jot down your thoughts. The book contains fifty weeks of devotions in addition to a set of devotions for the week of Christmas and for Holy Week, the week before Easter. You'll find these special holiday devotions at the back of the book.

God has a destiny in store for you. Let's get going on your journey.

DEVOTIONS FOR

Winter

Week One

MONDAY - What God Requires

THE TEXT: *"What does the Lord require of you but to do justice, and to love kindness, and to walk humbly with your God?" (Micah 6:8).*

THE TALK: Different people in your life require things from you. Your boss requires you to do your job and get to work on time. Your utility company requires you to pay your bills. Your government requires you to follow the law and pay taxes. But do you know what God requires of you? God wants our covenant relationship with Him to be demonstrated in our relationships with others. God wants us to do justice, valuing and doing what is right and fair. God wants us to love kindness, showing people around us compassion and mercy. He wants us to walk humbly with Him, remembering that God is God and we are not.

Three Things God Requires:

1. *Do justice.*

2. *Love mercy.*

3. *Walk humbly.*

THE TAKEAWAY: Demonstrate your relationship with God in how you treat those around you.

TUESDAY - Align Your Life

THE TEXT: *"And he answered, 'You shall love the Lord your God with all your heart and with all your soul and with all* *your strength and with all your mind, and your neighbor as yourself'" (Luke 10:27).*

THE TALK: Jesus said that loving God and loving others are the two most important commandments in the law. God wants us to love Him with everything that is in us. We love God with our hearts and emotions. We love God with our souls as we worship Him and surrender to His will. We love God with our strength and honor Him with our physical bodies. We love God with our minds by learning to think about the world the way God does. And as we learn to love God, our love for God overflows into our love for those around us. When we get these two things right—loving God and loving others—everything else falls into place.

Two Priorities to Align Your Life:

1. Love God.

2. Love people.

THE TAKEAWAY: Love God and love other people. Getting these two priorities right brings the rest of your life into alignment.

WEDNESDAY - Get Your Relationships Unstuck

THE TEXT: *"If possible, so far as it depends on you, live peaceably with all" (Romans 12:18).*

THE TALK: Have you ever been in a relationship that seems stuck? For whatever reason, you can't get along with this other person. You say things, and he takes them the wrong way. You make an innocent mistake, and he insists it must have been personal. And you find yourself accusing, sniping back, and complaining just as much as they do.

Romans 12:18 tells us how to break the cycle. As far as it depends on you, do what you can to live at peace. You can't control their actions or change their behavior, so stop trying. Trying to change other people only sets you up for frustration and failure. But you can change yourself. What if when they said something mean, you just held your tongue? If you looked for opportunities to serve them and be kind? I'm not talking about being a doormat or putting yourself in danger. Sometimes we must be the first to put our weapons down.

Three Ways to Get Your Relationship Unstuck:

1. *Stop trying to change them.*

2. *Start trying to change yourself.*

3. *Do what is in your power to live at peace.*

THE TAKEAWAY: Do what you can to live at peace and see if the other person will meet you there.

THURSDAY - Transformed, Not Conformed

THE TEXT: *"Do not be conformed to this world, but be transformed by the renewal of your mind"* (Romans 12:2).

THE TALK: If we want to know what God wants, we need to let our minds be transformed and renewed by reading Scripture. We need to be in the Word every day. Not just reading the Bible, but asking God how what we're reading should make a difference in our lives. Because I've read this passage, what behavior do I need to change? What sin do I need to confess? What should be different about my finances, my relationships, and my job because of what I've read in God's Word today? As we feast on Scripture, we learn to think about the world the way God thinks. That transformation enables us to know God's will and put it into practice in our lives.

Three Ways to Know and Do God's Will:

1. *Devote time to reading God's Word.*

2. *Let Scripture renew your mind.*

3. *Let your renewed mind transform you.*

THE TAKEAWAY: Transform and renew your mind by reading God's Word and letting it make a difference in your life.

FRIDAY - Destiny

THE TEXT: *"Your eyes saw my unformed substance. In your book were written, every one of them, the days that were formed for me" (Psalm 139:16).*

THE TALK: God has a destiny for you. All the days of your life were written in God's book before you even came to be. To find your destiny, you need to know your directions and your director. Let God determine the course of your life. Don't tell God where you want to go—ask God who He wants you to be. Make God the director of your life, and He will guide you into your destiny.

Three Ways to Find Your Destiny:

1. *Determine your direction.*

2. *Determine your director.*

3. *Let God guide you into your destiny.*

THE TAKEAWAY: Let God lead you in His direction and into your divinely-appointed destiny.

WEEKEND REFLECTION - Walk Wisely

"Look carefully then how you walk, not as unwise but as wise, making the best use of the time, because the days are evil" (Ephesians 5:15-16).

❋

FOR REFLECTION: God wants us to walk wisely, using our time well because the days are short. How have you used your time this week? Have you walked wisely? Have you invested your days in loving God and loving others? Have you sought to do what pleases God? Ask God to show you how you can honor Him with your time as you begin a new week.

_____

_____

_____

_____

_____

_____

_____

_____

_____

_____

_____

_____

_____

_____

_____

_____

_____

Week Two

MONDAY - Becoming One

THE TEXT: *"There is neither Jew nor Greek, there is neither slave nor free, there is no male and female, for you are all one in Christ Jesus" (Galatians 3:28).*

THE TALK: Rigid social rules separated people in the New Testament world. Jew from Greek. Slave from free. Male from female. Paul reminded the Galatian church that the way things were now was not the way they always had to be. Christ had made them one. Male, female, slave, free, Jew, and Greek— they all stood equally in need of God's grace. God brought people together despite their differences and made them one, uniting them as they followed Jesus Christ as Lord.

Three Ways to Pursue Equality:

1. *Remember that the way things are is not the way they always have to be.*

2. *Remember that we are all equally in need of grace.*

3. *Radically celebrate diversity, praising the God who has made us one.*

THE TAKEAWAY: Show respect and honor for others, thanking God for the diversity of the body of Christ.

TUESDAY - Diversity is Key

THE TEXT: *"And he called to him his twelve disciples and gave them authority . . . The names of the twelve apostles are these: first, Simon (who is called Peter) and Andrew his brother;*

James the son of Zebedee, and John his brother; Philip and Bartholomew; Thomas and Matthew the tax collector; James the son of Alphaeus, and Thaddaeus; Simon the Zealot, and Judas Iscariot, who betrayed him" (Matthew 10:1-4).

THE TALK: The diverse group of disciples Jesus assembled should have fractured at the seams. They were politically, religiously, and culturally diverse. But Jesus called them to himself. He spent time with them. He discipled them. He gave them opportunities to lead—and to fail. When Jesus was done with them, they turned the world upside down.

There is power in diversity. When we come together despite our differences, united in Christ's name, nothing can stand in our way. In Christ, the differences that once divided us give us the power to turn the world upside down.

Three Ways to Demonstrate the Power in Diversity:

1. Be open to genuinely getting to know others.

2. Remember God has made us different on purpose.

3. Look for the ways our difference gives us power.

THE TAKEAWAY: Christ makes our differences into tools of unity rather than sources of division.

WEDNESDAY - Breaking Racial Barriers

THE TEXT: *"And he had to pass through Samaria" (John 4:4).*

THE TALK: Jews and Samaritans hated one another. The Samaritans were the remnants of the peoples Assyria settled in the land when Israel was in exile. The Jews thought of them as half-breeds and looked down on the altered form of Judaism the Samaritans adopted. Most Jews chose to go out of their way to avoid Samaria.

But Jesus had to go through Samaria. Jesus was seeking worshippers, and there was a woman in Samaria who was looking for Him—even if she didn't know it yet. Jesus went out of His comfort zone to meet her. She challenged Him. But Jesus challenged her right back. He went onto her turf to meet her where she was. Jesus changed her, and she changed her town. The entire community followed Jesus.

Three Ways to Break Racial Barriers:

1. *Get out of your comfort zone.*

2. *Meet people who will challenge you.*

3. *Seek to understand.*

THE TAKEAWAY: To bring change, we have to be willing to get out of our comfort zone, seek understanding, and meet people who challenge us so we can introduce them to Jesus.

THURSDAY - Crossing Racial Divides

THE TEXT: *"And while Peter was pondering the vision, the Spirit said to him, 'Behold, three men are looking for you. Rise up and go down and accompany them without hesitation, for I have sent them'"* (Acts 10:19-20).

THE TALK: The first believers were Jewish. Jews thought of Gentiles (non-Jews) as unclean and immoral. Though Jesus had told the disciples to take the gospel to all peoples, it took them a while to understand they were actually supposed to do it. God sent Peter a vision and a man named Cornelius to remind Peter of the Father's heart: All nations. All tribes. All tongues. All peoples reconciled to himself—and to each other.

God still calls us to cross racial divides. But like Peter, we have to deal with our own hearts first. The racial barrier wasn't Cornelius' problem. It was Peter's. He had to deal with his heart, his ignorance, and his fear. Only then was he ready to do what God had called him to do: reach the world with the gospel.

Three Ways to Cross the Racial Divide:

1. *Deal with your heart.*

2. *Deal with your ignorance.*

3. *Deal with your fear.*

THE TAKEAWAY: To cross racial divides, examine yourself for racism—not the other person. Take care of your own heart so you can reach the world with the gospel.

FRIDAY - Answering Opposition to Activism

THE TEXT: *"Miriam and Aaron spoke against Moses because of the Cushite woman whom he had married, for he had married a Cushite woman" (Numbers 12:1).*

THE TALK: Miriam and Aaron, Moses' sister and brother, started speaking out against Moses because he had married a Cushite black woman—a non-Jew. Their complaints were based on false perceptions. They perceived that Moses' marriage meant they would lose their place of privilege. They perceived that they were losing their power. And so they responded by trying to bring Moses down. They were angry because of the nationality of Moses' wife.

When we move toward justice and start to bring down the forces of racism and oppression, some people are going to perceive that they're losing something and be unhappy about it. Opposition is the cost of doing what is right. But like Moses, we can trust God to defend us. Moses was the victim, but he still prayed for his oppressor. That's the attitude we need as we bring change in our culture.

❄

Three Ways to Answer Opposition:

1. *Confront false perceptions.*

2. *Trust God to defend you.*

3. *Pray for your oppressors.*

THE TAKEAWAY: Lead the way in being the change you want to see. Pray for those who oppose you. God will defend you.

WEEKEND REFLECTION - Tearing Down Walls

"For he himself is our peace, who has made the two groups one and has destroyed the barrier, the dividing wall of hostility" (Ephesians 2:14).

FOR REFLECTION: Christ is the peacemaker who has torn down the barriers and dividing walls to make us one. How have you seen God tear down the barriers and dividing walls in your life? What walls still exist between you and others? Ask God to tear them down.

_____

_____

_____

_____

_____

_____

_____

_____

_____

Week Three

MONDAY - Conquer the Day

THE TEXT: *"No, in all these things we are more than conquerors through him who loved us"* *(Romans 8:37).*

THE TALK: We are in a spiritual battle. Every morning when your feet hit the floor, you are getting ready to engage in battle. Satan hurls his arsenal at us, but we are not victims. We are conquerors.

Here's what you need to know to be victorious. First, you need to know your enemy. Satan wants to steal your worship and destroy your testimony. But he is already defeated. The key to defeating Satan is knowing who you are. Christ is in you. Through His death and resurrection, Jesus Christ triumphed over Satan and all the forces of evil. We share in His victory. Finally, you have to know your weapons. We don't fight like the world does. The tools of our warfare are spiritual, not carnal. Righteousness. Holiness. Truth. Prayer. These are the weapons God gives us to bring about the victory.

Three Tools for Victory:

1. *Know your enemy.*

2. *Know yourself.*

3. *Know your weaponry.*

THE TAKEAWAY: Satan may fight against you, but through Jesus you have already won. Take up your weapons and live like the conqueror you are.

TUESDAY - A Greater Power

THE TEXT: *"Now to him who is able to do far more abundantly than all that we ask or think, according to the power at work within us"* (Ephesians 3:20).

THE TALK: Movies love telling the stories of powerful people—superheroes like Wonder Woman, Superman, Iron Man, and Hulk. We flock to these movies because they invite us to imagine being stronger, smarter, and more powerful than we are. But we have a power greater than Superman ever dreamed of. The same power that raised Jesus from the dead—the resurrection power of the Holy Spirit—is at work in us. And through that power God is able to do more abundantly than anything we could ask or imagine. Stop walking around acting like you're already defeated. God's resurrection power is at work in you. You've already won.

Three Types of Power:

1. *You have God's resurrection power.*

2. *You have God's abundant power.*

3. *You have God's greater power.*

THE TAKEAWAY: You are powerful because God's power is at work in you.

WEDNESDAY - Overcoming the World

THE TEXT: *"Little children, you are from God and have overcome them, for he who is in you is greater than he who is in the world"* (1 John 4:4).

THE TALK: Do you ever feel like it's opposite day? Children sometimes declare that today is "opposite day"—a day when *yes* means *no*, *up* means *down*, and *day* means *night*. Our world can seem like opposite day gone wrong. What we call truth, they call a lie. What we call good, they call bad. What we call profane, they insist is worthy of respect. Even some who call themselves Christians have embraced this upside down world. But He who is in us is greater than the world. We will face opposition, but we have already overcome because Jesus is greater. We are not from this world. We are from God, and we will triumph because Jesus has already won.

Three Truths to Remember:

1. *You are not from this world.*

2. *You belong to God.*

3. *You will triumph because Jesus has already won.*

THE TAKEAWAY: Christ's power in us ensures that we will overcome.

THURSDAY - Power Drains

THE TEXT: *"And she said, 'The Philistines are upon you, Samson!' And he awoke from his sleep and said, 'I will go out as at other times and shake myself free.' But he did not know that the Lord had left him" (Judges 16:20).*

THE TALK: God chose Samson to deliver Israel from the Philistines. Set apart from birth, he was never to drink alcohol or to cut his hair. God blessed Samson with supernatural strength.

Samson used his strength to fight the Philistines, but Samson was as foolish as he was strong. He fell in love with a woman named Delilah. The Philistines bribed her to find out the secret of Samson's strength, and while he was asleep she called someone to shave his hair. Samson had exchanged God's promise for the world's pleasure, and his strength left him. He didn't know his power was gone until he tried to use it; Samson then discovered his exchange had left him powerless.

We need to avoid drains on our spiritual power. Sin, relationships, overcommitment, and not taking time for self-care can all drain our power. When we feel weak, we need to assess what's going on. Identify the source of the power drain, remove it, and recharge by reconnecting with God.

Three Steps to Regain Your Power:

1. *Identify the power drains in your life.*

2. *Get rid of things that drain your power.*

3. *Recharge by reconnecting with God.*

THE TAKEAWAY: Don't tolerate power drains in your life. Remove them and recharge by reconnecting with God.

FRIDAY - Freed to Obey

THE TEXT: *"What shall we say then? Are we to continue in sin that grace may abound? By no means! How can we who died to sin still live in it?" (Romans 6:1-2).*

THE TALK: Grace is a life preserver for the drowning, not a permission slip to continue sinning. Grace is what rescues us from the penalty of our sin. There are different types of sin. We can miss the mark or step over the line, accidentally falling into sin. Or we can commit transgressions—deliberate acts of disobedience. Regardless, sin comes with a penalty: death. Grace removes the penalty and sets us free so that we don't have to keep on sinning. We are freed to live obediently to God. Don't cheapen God's grace by continuing in sin. Live as the free and obedient person God has made you to be.

Three Responses to Grace:

1. *Grace frees you to be obedient.*

2. *Don't cheapen God's grace by continuing to sin.*

3. *Live like the free people God has made you to be.*

THE TAKEAWAY: God's grace frees you for obedience. Walk in your freedom.

WEEKEND REFLECTION – Under His Authority

"And Jesus came and said to them, 'All authority in heaven and on earth has been given to me'" (Matthew 28:18).

FOR REFLECTION: All authority on heaven and earth belong to Jesus. We live under His authority and are agents in charge of extending His kingdom on earth. How are you seeing Christ's authority and power demonstrated in your life? What areas of your life do you need to bring under His authority?

_____

_____

_____

_____

_____

_____

_____

_____

_____

_____

_____

Week Four

MONDAY - Favor Find Me, Part 1

THE TEXT: *"Abel also brought of the firstborn of his flock and of their fat portions. And the Lord had regard for Abel and his offering"* (Genesis 4:4).

THE TALK: Cain and Abel, the sons of Adam and Eve, both brought offerings to the Lord. Cain brought some of the produce of the field, but Abel brought the firstborn of his flock. God showed Abel favor because he brought a first fruit offering of his flock. He didn't wait till all the lambs gave birth and keep the best for himself. Abel gave God the very first of his increase, trusting that God would deliver the rest. We are also to follow Abel's example of bringing our first and best to God. Don't give God your leftovers. Begin your week with worship. Read your Bible and pray as soon as your feet hit the floor in the morning. Let your tithe check be the first check you write. Give God your first fruits, and He will give you favor.

Giving the First Fruits:

1. *God gave His first fruits to us: Jesus.*

2. *God commands us to give Him our first fruits.*

3. *God guarantees His favor when we give Him our first and best.*

THE TAKEAWAY: Give God your first fruits so you will be blessed and bear more fruit.

TUESDAY - Favor Find Me, Part 2

THE TEXT: *"And the Lord had regard for Abel and his offering, but for Cain and his offering he had no regard. So Cain was very angry, and his face fell"* (Genesis 4:4-5).

THE TALK: God responded with favor to Abel's offering, but He didn't accept Cain's. Cain's actions reveal that the problem wasn't with Cain's offering but with Cain's heart. Cain was angry that God had accepted Abel's offering and not his, and so Cain killed Abel. But Abel's blood cried out to God from the ground, and God brought justice. Favor will attract haters—people who don't understand why God shows you favor, who are jealous that He does, and who may try to destroy you to stop God from putting favor on your life. But favor speaks. Even in your absence, God's favor will be evident. No one can stop God's favor from getting to you. Don't let the haters stop you. Make the first move. Bring God your first fruits, and favor will find you.

When Haters Hate:

1. *Do what is right and give God your best.*

2. *Let God deal with the haters.*

3. *Favor will find you.*

THE TAKEAWAY: Don't fear the haters. Bring God your first fruits and He will show you favor.

WEDNESDAY - Family First

THE TEXT: *"And when they were in the field, Cain rose up against his brother Abel and killed him"* (Genesis 4:8).

THE TALK: I teared up as I watched President Obama speak about his love for his family during his farewell address as he left the White House. During his two terms as president, we didn't see any drama from his family. He, Michelle, and their daughters presented a picture of a solid family where the parents love each other and love their children. I want a family like that. But truthfully, all families have drama. It started at the very beginning with the very first family. Adam and Eve ate the forbidden fruit and introduced sin into the world. Family drama came with it. The first murder happened within the first family as Cain killed his brother Abel. Yet God was gracious. He extended grace even to Cain, though Cain refused to receive it. And God gave grace to Adam and Eve by blessing them with another child: Seth. Through Seth's birth, God continued to offer redemption to the fallen family. It was Seth's family line that eventually led to Jesus. Let God's grace redeem your family drama, too.

Dealing with Family Drama:

1. *Consider the conflict. How did the drama start in your family?*

2. *Respond with love. Be the person who originates love in your family.*

3. *Accept God's grace and keep moving forward.*

THE TAKEAWAY: Let God's grace redeem your family drama. Receive His offering of grace.

THURSDAY - Finish Your Story

THE TEXT: *"And I am sure of this, that he who began a good work in you will bring it to completion at the day of Jesus Christ" (Philippians 1:6).*

THE TALK: Paul wrote these words while he was in a Roman jail chained between two members of Caesar's Praetorian Guard. Even in these conditions Paul wrote confidently about God's plans for the Philippian church. When you feel discouraged about your story, remember Paul. You are in control of your narrative. It's not about what happens to you—it's about how you respond. Don't try to copy anyone else's story. Know God and His plans for you, and be resolute in writing down your story—no one else's. Be confident no matter your circumstances. God will finish His story in you.

Writing the Story:

1. *It's not your circumstances that matter, it's how you respond.*

2. *Be original. Don't copy someone else's story. Write your own.*

3. *Know God and believe His promise. He will complete your story.*

THE TAKEAWAY: Your story is incomplete because it is not finished. Be patient. God will finish what He started in you.

FRIDAY - Keep Hope Alive

THE TEXT: *"And hope does not put us to shame, because God's love has been poured into our hearts through the Holy Spirit who has been given to us"* (Romans 5:5).

THE TALK: We have a hope that never disappoints and never lets us down. Our hope is built on the surety of the resurrection, the promise of Christ's coming, and the power of the Holy Spirit. Hope is the emotion of faith. Faith is not a feeling, but it needs hope to work. Without hope of our future with God, our faith will fail. We hope in more than the vagaries of fate. We hope in the promise of eternal life in Christ's presence for all eternity, and that hope will never let us down.

Keep Hoping:

1. *Keep hoping because your faith needs hope to work.*

2. *Keep hoping because hope keeps you faithful, not fatalistic.*

3. *Keep hoping because your hope in Christ won't put you to shame.*

THE TAKEAWAY: Christ is your source of hope. Hope in Him.

WEEKEND REFLECTION

"And it shall come to pass afterward, that I will pour out my Spirit on all flesh; your sons and your daughters shall prophesy, your old men will dream dreams, and your young men shall see visions" (Joel 2:28).

FOR REFLECTION: God wants His people to be a people of vision. Men and women, young and old—we are meant to be a visionary people through the power of the Spirit. What vision has God given you? Are you being true to that vision? Ask God to give you His vision for your life and ministry.

_____

_____

_____

_____

_____

_____

_____

_____

Week Five

MONDAY - Under Wraps

THE TEXT: *"So his brothers said to him, 'Leave here and go to Judea, that your disciples also may see the works you are doing'"* (John 7:3).

THE TALK: Jesus faced opposition even from within His own family. Jesus was preaching in Galilee. Jesus' brothers—who did not believe in Him—told Him to go into Judea and minister publicly. But it wasn't yet His time. Jesus knew the cross was coming, but He was still in a season of ministry and proclamation. He had to be obedient to a higher calling.

We also need to know the seasons we are in. Sometimes it is our season to boldly speak the truth and face the opposition when it comes. Sometimes it is our season to wait in obscurity, letting God prepare us for what He has in store. There will be people in our lives who try to define our seasons for us—telling us to speak up when we need to be quiet or to sit down when we need to stand up. But it is our job to be faithful and obedient in the season God has given us. Listen to God's voice, not the voices of people who don't believe.

Three Ways to Know Your Season:

1. *Let God define your season.*

2. *Focus on pleasing God, not others.*

3. *Stay faithful to God's calling.*

THE TAKEAWAY: Know the season you're in and be faithful to that calling.

❄

TUESDAY - Just Be Yourself

THE TEXT: *"Jesus answered, 'Even if I do bear witness about myself, my testimony is true, for I know where I came from and where I am going, but you do not know where I come from or where I am going'"* (John 8:14).

THE TALK: When Jesus said He was the light of the world, the Pharisees refused to believe Him. They settled for petty quibbling over whether Jesus had the legal authority to testify about himself. But Jesus knew that His authority was greater than any human witness. Both God the Father and God the Son testified about who Jesus was. No other witnesses were needed.

God has the authority to say who you are. If God says you're forgiven, you're forgiven. If God says you're an overcomer, you're an overcomer. If God says you're a new creation, then that's who you are. Don't let other people determine your identity. Root yourself in the knowledge of who God has declared you to be.

Three Truths about Your Identity:

1. *God determines your identity.*

2. *Other people's responses don't change your identity.*

3. *Your job is to live like the person God has made you to be.*

THE TAKEAWAY: God has the authority to declare your identity. His word on you is the only one that matters.

WEDNESDAY - Being Your Best Self

THE TEXT: *"The devil said to him, 'If you are the Son of God, command this stone to become bread'"* (Luke 4:3).

THE TALK: During Jesus' temptation, Satan's first challenge was to Jesus' identity. *"If* you are the Son of God. . ." (emphasis added). Satan was challenging Jesus to prove His identity, but Jesus had no need to prove anything. He knew who He was. His identity was best demonstrated in continued dependence on the Father.

Satan still challenges us at the point of our identity. He tempts us to define ourselves outside of our relationship with God. But once we set our identity and worth on an outside source, we have turned away from who God has created us to be. God made us in His image that we would be like Him. We are our truest selves when we are most like Jesus. We find our identity by living in relationship with and dependence on the Father.

How to be Your Best Self:

1. *Remember that you are made in God's image.*

2. *Find your identity in your relationship with the Father.*

3. *You are your best self when you are most like Jesus.*

THE TAKEAWAY: Your most authentic self is found in living the most like Jesus.

THURSDAY - Don't Derail Your Destiny

THE TEXT: *"For I know the plans I have for you, declares the Lord, plans for welfare and not for evil, to give you a future and a hope" (Jeremiah 29:11).*

THE TALK: God spoke these words through the prophet Jeremiah during one of his people's darkest hours. The people of Judah were in exile in Babylon. But despite their difficulty, God promised that He had good plans for them—plans to give them a future and a hope.

Difficulty doesn't mean you don't have a destiny. Persevere and hold on to hope. God's plans for you are always good. Keep moving forward into the destiny God has waiting for you.

How to Respond to Difficulty:

1. *Don't let difficulty make you give up on your destiny.*

2. *Remember that God's plans for you are always good.*

3. *Persevere and move forward into your God-given destiny.*

THE TAKEAWAY: Difficulty doesn't have to derail your destiny. God's plans for you include a future and a hope.

FRIDAY - Abundant Life

THE TEXT: *"The thief comes only to steal and kill and destroy. I came that they may have life and have it abundantly"* (John 10:10).

THE TALK: Shepherds care for their sheep. They move them around frequently to give them good pastures for grazing. They protect them from predators. They treat their diseases and injuries. Good shepherds want their sheep to prosper because the sheep prosper the shepherd.

Jesus' promise of abundant life is rooted in His identity as the Good Shepherd. He cares for us so that we can live abundantly. Satan wants to destroy us, but Jesus wants us to prosper. He meets our needs. He protects us from attack. He heals our wounds. He cares for us because we are valuable to Him.

Three Truths about Your Shepherd:

1. *You are valuable to the Shepherd*

2. *Your Shepherd cares for you.*

3. *Your Shepherd wants you to prosper.*

THE TAKEAWAY: I live well because I am priceless to the Shepherd.

WEEKEND REFLECTION

"See what kind of love the Father has given to us, that we should be called children of God; and so we are" (1 John 3:1).

FOR REFLECTION: God is not stingy with His love. He lavishes it on us, calling us His children. How has God shown you His lavish love this week? What difference does it make to know that you are a beloved child of God? Ask God to help you base your identity on the reality of God's love for you.

_____

_____

_____

_____

_____

_____

_____

_____

_____

_____

_____

_____

_____

_____

Week Six

MONDAY - Unconditional Love

THE TEXT: *"For God so loved the world, that he gave his only Son, that whoever believes in him should not perish but have eternal life" (John 3:16).*

THE TALK: The New Testament uses different words to describe different kinds of love. The word used in John 3:16 is *agape. Agape* describes God's faithful, sacrificial, covenant love.

Agape love is not a feeling. It is an action. Agape love describes the willingness to sacrifice and suffer for someone else's good. It is unconditional, loving without expectation of return. God loved us enough to send His only Son, rescuing us from death and giving us the gift of eternal life. You are loved. God loves you perfectly, sacrificially, and unconditionally. Will you give Him your love in return?

Responding to God's Unconditional Love:

1. *Love is an action, not a feeling.*

2. *God showed His love by giving you Jesus.*

3. *Show your love for God by giving Him your heart.*

THE TAKEAWAY: God gave you Jesus. Give Him your heart.

TUESDAY - Love My Enemies?

THE TEXT: *"Love your enemies and pray for those who persecute you, so that you may be sons of your Father who is in heaven" (Matthew 5:44-45).*

THE TALK: Loving your enemies sounds easy until you have one. Most of us don't want to love our enemies. We want to get even. But Jesus tells us to love our enemies. Why?

This command to love our enemies protects our own hearts. Hatred and bitterness poison the soul. Forgiveness heals. But loving our enemies doesn't mean putting ourselves at risk. Sometimes we have to love from a distance. We can show kindness without allowing them full access to our lives and hearts. The most important way we can love them is by giving them Jesus—doing what we can safely and sanely do to point them to Jesus. And as we show them Jesus, Jesus shows himself to us.

Three Ways to Love Your Enemies:

1. *Forgive them.*

2. *Pray for them.*

3. *Show them Jesus.*

THE TAKEAWAY: Love your enemies by praying for them and showing them Jesus.

WEDNESDAY - Love Trumps Fear

THE TEXT: *"There is no fear in love, but perfect love casts out fear. For fear has to do with punishment, and whoever fears has not been perfected in love"* (1 John 4:18).

THE TALK: Sometimes we look at God like He's Lucy with Charlie Brown's football—holding out a promise in front of us only to yank it away at the last second, leaving us lying flat on the ground. But God doesn't treat us that way. He loves us. If we are in Christ, we don't have to fear God's punishment. He has already given us His grace. When we're afraid, we don't need to look into ourselves to find courage. We need to look to the one who has loved us perfectly: Jesus. As we fall deeper in love with Jesus, His love fills us till there's no room left for fear. We don't have to fear when we've been made perfect in God's love.

How to Overcome Fear:

1. *Focus your gaze on God.*

2. *Fall deeper in love with God.*

3. *Demonstrate your love for God.*

THE TAKEAWAY: When you're afraid, fall deeper in love with Jesus. Love triumphs over fear.

THURSDAY - Love Looks Like Obedience

THE TEXT: *"If you love me, you will keep my commandments"* (John 15:13).

THE TALK: In Scripture, love looks like obedience. Love for God should be more than a feeling. Getting a spiritual high from a powerful service or your favorite worship song doesn't prove your love for God. Your obedience does. Do you speak truth? Give generously? Pursue purity? Honor your parents? Love others? Pray for your enemies? Do you love God consistently, or only when it is convenient for you? If you love God, then obey Him. Get in the Word and do what it says. Your obedience shows your love.

Three Ways to Show Love for God:

1. *Learn what God commands.*

2. *Love what God loves.*

3. *Do what God says to do.*

THE TAKEAWAY: Your obedience to God demonstrates your love for God.

❄

FRIDAY - How Are You Loving?

THE TEXT: *"This is my commandment: that you love one another as I have loved you" (John 15:12).*

THE TALK: On the last night Jesus spent with His disciples, Jesus gave them one final commandment: love one another. Jesus wanted the disciples to love one another as He had loved them. Jesus had served them. He had been patient with them. And in a few short hours, He would give His life for them. Jesus wanted the disciples to follow His example of love.

We are also meant to love like Jesus. Sacrificially. Unconditionally. Loving in a way that seeks the other person's best, always looking for ways to point them to the Father. If you want to know how to love, look at Jesus.

How to Love Like Jesus:

1. *Commit yourself to service and sacrifice.*

2. *Consider the other person's best interests.*

3. *Carry them to the Father.*

THE TAKEAWAY: Jesus is our example of how to love. We are to love like Jesus.

WEEKEND REFLECTION

"By this all people will know that you are my disciples, if you have love for one another" (John 14:35).

FOR REFLECTION: Jesus said that the world will know we are His disciples if we love one another. Real love—Jesus' kind of love—can't be hidden or ignored. It shows. How have your actions this week demonstrated Jesus' kind of love? Who needs you to show them Jesus' love? What is one action step you could take to show them love? Ask God for wisdom and strength to love like Jesus.

Week Seven

MONDAY - How to Get Through the Storm

THE TEXT: *"The sea became rough because a strong wind was blowing" (John 6:18).*

THE TALK: After the feeding of the five thousand, the disciples got into a boat to cross to the other side of the Sea of Galilee. The geography of the mountains surrounding the sea and the way they funnel the wind can produce strong storms in a short amount of time. As the disciples tried to cross the sea, one of these strong storms suddenly blew up and the sea became rough. The disciples were afraid, but Jesus came out to them walking on the water. He had been watching all along. The disciples were scared of the storm, but the storm was what brought Jesus to them. And if we'll let them, the storms in our life can be what brings Jesus to us, too.

How to Get Through a Storm:

1. *You can't always tell storms are coming. Don't get caught off guard when they do.*

2. *Don't stop in the middle of the storm. Keep forging ahead to the other side.*

3. *Take courage. Jesus is watching, and He will come to you.*

THE TAKEAWAY: Don't let the storm stop you. It's there to bring Jesus to you.

TUESDAY - Jesus, the Boat, and You

THE TEXT: *"And Peter answered him, 'Lord, if it is you, command me to come to you on the water'" (Matthew 14:28).*

THE TALK: When the disciples saw Jesus walking on the water, they were afraid. They didn't recognize it was Jesus—they thought it was a ghost! Jesus assured the disciples it was Him. Peter told Jesus, "if it is you, command me to come to you."

Peter wanted proof it was really Jesus. Sometimes we do, too. But if Jesus has told you He will be with you, then He will be. Stop worrying and trust Him. There's no storm so great that Jesus can't reach you. He's there. Look out across the water—He's coming to you.

Three Tools for Peace in the Storm:

1. Stop worrying. Jesus is with you.

2. Get to the other side. Do what God told you to do.

3. Look out. Jesus is coming to you.

THE TAKEAWAY: No storm can stop Jesus from getting to you. Trust Him. He's already there.

WEDNESDAY - Beware of Faith Killers

THE TEXT: *"Lord, if it is you, command me to come to you on the water" (Matthew 14:28).*

THE TALK: Satan doesn't want your stuff. He may target your health, your family, or your finances, but those things are only openings to help him reach his real goal. What Satan really wants is your faith. That's why we have to watch out for faith killers like inactivity, fear, and losing focus. We can see all three of these faith killers at work in this story. As Jesus came walking through the storm, the disciples' inactivity killed their faith. Peter was the only disciple who activated his faith and was willing to step out on the water. Those who remained in the boat lost the chance to experience the power of faith. But their fear also dealt their faith a death blow. The disciples were afraid of the storm and their fear kept them from recognizing

Jesus. While Peter activated his faith by stepping out on the water, lack of focus killed it. Peter's faith let him walk on the water with Jesus, but when he took his eyes off Jesus and looked at the storm, he started to sink. Fear, inactivity, and lack of focus killed the disciples' faith. Be on guard that they don't kill yours.

Three Faith Killers to Avoid:

1. *Inactivity. Act on your faith if you want it to grow.*

2. *Fear. Find courage in Jesus' nearness.*

3. *Lack of focus. Fix your eyes on Jesus and don't look away.*

THE TAKEAWAY: Avoid faith killers by fixing your eyes on Jesus.

THURSDAY - Riding Out the Storm

THE TEXT: *"And [Jesus] awoke and rebuked the wind and said to the sea, 'Peace! Be still! And the wind ceased, and there was a great calm'"* (Mark 4:39).

THE TALK: Jesus and His disciples faced more than one storm on the Sea of Galilee. One night as Jesus and His disciples crossed the sea together, a strong storm came up and the boat was nearly capsized. The disciples looked for Jesus but He was asleep. The disciples woke Jesus up, not understanding how He could sleep when their lives were at risk. Jesus calmed the storm and challenged the disciples' faith.

The storms in your life can't swamp you if Jesus is with you. Ride out the storm by doing what He has told you to do. Don't quit. Keep obeying and keep moving forward till you get to the other side. Jesus is more powerful than the storms in your life. He'll see you through.

Three Ways to Ride Out the Storm:

1. *Keep doing what God has told you to do.*

2. *Keep praising Jesus, who is stronger than the storm.*

3. *Keep reminding yourself that you're safe because Jesus is with you.*

THE TAKEAWAY: When storms come, don't be afraid. Keep on obeying and remember you are safe because Jesus is with you.

FRIDAY - The Safety of Stillness

THE TEXT: *"Be still and know that I am God. I will be exalted among the nations, I will be exalted in the earth!" (Psalm 46:10).*

THE TALK: Stillness can be safety. Have you ever watched what a rabbit does when it senses a predator nearby? It freezes. Being still keeps the rabbit from drawing attention and helps it blend in with its surroundings. In the same way, when we face trouble, sometimes all we need is to be still. Instead of running around looking for our own solutions, we need to wait quietly on God's direction. God is in charge, working for our good and His glory. Our stillness gives God a chance to show how great He is.

Three Ways to Practice Stillness:

1. *Stop looking for your own solutions.*

2. *Wait quietly on God's direction.*

3. *Give God a chance to show His greatness.*

THE TAKEAWAY: Be still and let God show His greatness in your life.

WEEKEND REFLECTION

"And he is before all things, and in him all things hold together" (Colossians 1:17).

FOR REFLECTION: Physicists can tell you about the forces that hold atoms together, but the Bible gives a greater answer. Christ was before all things, created all things, and holds all things together. Our world is sustained and held together by Christ's sovereignty and will. When it feels like the world is falling apart, how does it help you to know Christ is holding it together? How have you seen God's power to hold things together demonstrated in your life? Ask God to help you rest in the confidence that your world is safe in His hands.

_____

_____

_____

_____

_____

_____

_____

_____

_____

_____

_____

_____

_____

Week Eight

MONDAY - On Your Own

THE TEXT: *"And David was deeply distressed, for the people spoke of stoning him, because all the people were bitter in soul, each for his sons and daughters. But David strengthened himself in the Lord." (1 Samuel 30:6)*

THE TALK: An enemy had attacked David's base camp, burning the city with fire and carrying the women and children into captivity. The people blamed David and were ready to stone him. But David found his strength in the Lord. He led his men into battle and rescued all those who had been taken captive. Everything the enemy had taken was restored.

Sometimes what we tell ourselves matters more than what we do. David didn't sit around telling himself that he was already defeated. He found his strength in the Lord, and God gave him the power to rescue his people. We need to tell ourselves the truth. God is victorious. He is powerful. God is with us, and He is *for* us. Telling ourselves the truth helps us win the victory.

Three Things to Say to Yourself:

1. *Tell yourself the truth about who God is.*

2. *Tell yourself the truth about who you are.*

3. *Tell yourself the truth about what God is going to do.*

THE TAKEAWAY: Prepare for victory by telling yourself the truth about who God is and who you are to Him.

TUESDAY - Mirror the Change

THE TEXT: *"So whatever you wish that others would do to you, do also to them, for this is the Law and the Prophets"* (Matthew 7:12).

THE TALK: Everyone deserves dignity. When we're offended, angry, or hurt, we often want to dehumanize the people who are against us. If we can reduce them to a name or a label, we think it makes it okay for us to treat them as less than human. But Jesus says this is what we must not do. We have an obligation to treat the people around us with the dignity bestowed on them by the Creator. We have to be the change we want to see. If I mirror the image on my cell phone on a larger screen, I have to change the image on my phone to change the image on the screen. In the same way, we have to mirror the changes we want to see in society. If we want others to treat us with dignity, we have to mirror that change. It starts with me.

Three Ways to Mirror Change:

1. *See others as God's creation.*

2. *Treat everyone with equal dignity.*

3. *Be the change you want to see.*

THE TAKEAWAY: Treat others with dignity and mirror the change you want to see.

WEDNESDAY - Running Outta Cheeks

THE TEXT: *"But I say to you, do not resist the one who is evil. But if anyone slaps you on the right cheek, turn to him the other also"* (Matthew 5:39).

THE TALK: In the Sermon on the Mount, Jesus explained what it looks like to live as a citizen of the kingdom of God.

❄

Jesus called His followers to lay aside their right to retaliation. For a Jewish man, being struck on the cheek was an insult rather than an act of violence or aggression. Jesus was telling His followers not to escalate conflict with retaliation.

Turning the other cheek means not sinking to the other person's level when we are insulted or offended. It doesn't mean that we stop seeking justice. We can—and should— confront authorities for improper uses of power. But when others insult or demean us, we don't respond in kind. Our character should speak for itself.

Four Things to Do When You Run Out of Cheeks:

1. *Follow the kingdom standard.*

2. *Give up your right to retaliation.*

3. *Seek justice.*

4. *Let your character speak for itself.*

THE TAKEAWAY: We can reject retribution in order to speak for justice.

THURSDAY - Turning the Tables

THE TEXT: *"And he entered the table and began to drive out those who sold and those who bought in the temple, and he overturned the tables of the money-changers and the seats of those who sold pigeons" (Mark 11:15).*

THE TALK: Jesus was not silent in the face of injustice. The money changers and merchants in the tabernacle were cheating people and were preventing them from worshipping. Jesus took action against them.

What do we do when we have had enough of the injustice we see? We have options. We can form coalitions with people who may look different than we do but who share our concerns. We can protest unjust systems. We can participate in the civic process. Jesus' life was a living protest against injustice. Our lives can be as well.

Three Ways to Turn the Tables:

1. *Protest injustice wherever you find it.*

2. *Speak up for those who can't speak for themselves.*

3. *Form coalitions with people who share your concerns.*

THE TAKEAWAY: Let your life be a protest against injustice. Speak for those who cannot speak for themselves.

FRIDAY - The Path to Change

THE TEXT: *"First of all, then, I urge that supplications, prayers, intercessions, and thanksgivings be made for all people, for kings and all who are in high positions, that we may lead a peaceful and quiet life, godly and dignified in every way" (1 Timothy 2:1-2).*

THE TALK: Paul was not naïve about the corruption and injustice of the Roman government. And yet he still encouraged Christians to pray for kings and those in positions of authority. If Paul could urge Christians living under the thumb of Rome to pray for those in authority over them, should we do any less? If we want to live peaceful, quiet, dignified lives, we need to pray for our government officials—even the ones we disagree with or don't like. Engage with the political process. Vote. Speak out. But don't forget to pray.

Three Ways to Pray for Government Officials:

1. *Pray that God will direct their decisions.*

2. *Pray God will open their minds and hearts to truth.*

3. *Pray God will give them the courage and conviction to do what is right.*

THE TAKEAWAY: Change comes from prayer and action.

WEEKEND REFLECTION

"But Peter and John answered them, 'Whether it is right in the sight of God to listen to you rather than to God, you must judge, for we cannot but speak of what we have seen and heard'" (Acts 4:19-20).

FOR REFLECTION: After Peter and John were arrested, the Jewish authorities told them to stop speaking about Jesus. But Peter and John refused. They were accountable to a higher authority, and so they chose to obey God rather than men. Are you willing to accept the risks of obedience? In what circumstances might you have to choose to obey God over people? Ask God for the courage to stand when the time comes.

Week Nine

MONDAY - The Price is Right

THE TEXT: *"I am the good shepherd. The good shepherd lays down his life for the sheep" (John 10:11).*

THE TALK: In the biblical world, sheep were a measure of wealth. The number and quality of the sheep determined the value and net worth of the shepherd. As members of God's flock, we are priceless because of the great price that was paid for us. Jesus purchased us with His blood, and His investment in us was not a one-time purchase. God continues to invest in us so we can develop to our potential, proving valuable to the kingdom. We demonstrate our value by obeying who God is and reflecting His glory.

Three Measures of Your Worth:

1. *You are priceless because of the price paid for you.*

2. *God continues to invest in your growth.*

3. *Demonstrate your value by reflecting God's glory.*

THE TAKEAWAY: You are valuable because of the price Jesus paid for you. Demonstrate your value in how you live.

TUESDAY - How to Pass a Test

THE TEXT: *"Lifting up his eyes, then, and seeing that a large crowd was coming toward him, Jesus said to Philip, 'Where are we to buy bread, so that these people may eat?' He said this to test him, for he himself knew what he would do" (John 6:5-6).*

THE TALK: Jesus and His disciples had crossed to the other side of the Sea of Galilee, but a large crowd followed. Jesus knew the crowd would be hungry, so He asked the disciples where to find food. It was a test of the disciples' faith. But the disciples didn't understand. They worried about how much it would cost to buy bread for that many people. Jesus didn't shame them, He gave them an opportunity to grow.

Jesus doesn't test you to grade you but to grow you. When tests come, don't worry about not knowing the answers. The important thing is that you do answer. Show up for your tests without worrying about your grades. Jesus is testing you so you have a chance to grow.

Three Ways to Pass a Test:

1. *Remember that a test is an opportunity for growth.*

2. *Give your answer without worrying about your grade.*

3. *Follow your teacher's instructions and continue to grow.*

THE TAKEAWAY: The purpose of your test isn't to grade but to grow. Look for what God wants to grow in you.

WEDNESDAY - What are You Hungry For?

THE TEXT: *"Jesus said to them, 'My food is to do the will of him who sent me and to accomplish his work'"* (John 4:31).

THE TALK: Jesus knew that His true source of nourishment was doing the will of His Father. We need to follow Jesus' example of attending to our spiritual diet. Food is fuel, and we need to fill up on the spiritual fuel we need to prepare us for the week at hand. Take in the spiritual nourishment you need to fuel you for what God has in store: worship, service, and the Word. You can't thrive spiritually on an empty heart.

Three Ways to Feed Yourself Spiritually:

1. *Pay attention to what you eat. How are you nourishing yourself spiritually?*

2. *Eat a balanced diet of prayer, worship, service, and the Word.*

3. *Take time to eat.*

THE TAKEAWAY: Feed yourself on spiritual food.

THURSDAY - Choose to Believe

THE TEXT: *"Jesus said to him, 'Go; your son will live'"* (John 4:50).

THE TALK: One of the most difficult things you can do is to believe and then act on your belief, but that's what this man did. When he asked Jesus to heal his dying son, Jesus simply told him to go and that his son would live. The man received the word from Jesus and returned to his routine with no complaints, no questions, and no hesitation. He received his reward. Would you have done the same? Jesus' word is enough for us. When Jesus gives you a word, choose to believe.

How to Act on Your Belief:

1. *Listen. What is God saying to you?*

2. *Choose. Determine to believe God's Word.*

3. *Do. Base your actions on the security of God's promise.*

THE TAKEAWAY: Trust God's Word. God's promise is all you need.

FRIDAY - Better than Sacrifice

THE TEXT: *"Behold, to obey is better than sacrifice, and to listen than the fat of rams" (1 Samuel 15:22).*

THE TALK: God prefers obedience over sacrifice. It doesn't matter how much we give, how many hours we spend at church, or how much time we put into volunteering if we are ignoring God's commands. God wants us to obey Him. Just like athletes have to practice their fundamentals to win the victory, we have to practice our obedience if we want God to trust us with the greater things. Sacrifice isn't a substitute for obedience. God wants your heart.

Three Ways to Practice Your Obedience:

1. Resist the temptation to rationalize disobedience.

2. Ask God to reveal your sin.

3. Continually choose radical obedience.

THE TAKEAWAY: Obedience is better than sacrifice. Practice your obedience.

WEEKEND REFLECTION

"We have received grace and apostleship to bring about the obedience of faith for the sake of his name among all the nations" (Romans 1:5).

FOR REFLECTION: Faith is an expression of obedience. If God is who He says He is, believing Him and responding in faith is an act of obedience to His command. How has your life shown the obedience of faith this week? What is one area in which you need to grow in obedience? Ask God to help you live in faithful obedience to His Word.

Week Ten

MONDAY - Work the Plan

THE TEXT: *"I want you to know, brothers, that what has happened to me has really served to advance the gospel, so that it has become known throughout the whole imperial guard and to all the rest that my imprisonment is for Christ"* (Philippians 1:12-13).

THE TALK: Prison wasn't in Paul's plans, but it was part of God's plan. Though he had been falsely accused and unjustly imprisoned, Paul's imprisonment allowed him the opportunity to spread the gospel throughout Caesar's imperial guard and encouraged others to preach more boldly. God is not a God of chaos. Your circumstances may not make sense to you, but they can still be part of God's plan for your life. If you stay obedient and trust God to work through the process, the trials in your life can be the instruments God uses to point you to a better future. Don't fight it. Keep moving forward and see what God has planned for you.

Three Truths to Give You Strength in a Trial:

1. *God is our source of peace in times of trial.*

2. *Your plans may not include trials, but God's plans sometimes do.*

3. *Trials can be the instruments God uses to point you to a better future.*

THE TAKEAWAY: Don't fight your trials. Push forward into the future God has planned for you.

✻

TUESDAY - Stop Waiting

THE TEXT: *"One man was there who had been an invalid for thirty-eight years"* (John 5:5).

THE TALK: There was a pool in Jerusalem called Bethesda. Invalids lay in the colonnades surrounding the pool. People believed that at certain times an angel would stir the water and that the first person in the pool after the water moved would be healed. One man had been there waiting for his healing for thirty-eight years. Jesus asked the man if he wanted to be healed. The man said he did, but he had no one to help him into the water. Jesus told the man to get up, take up his bed, and walk. The man did so, and he was healed.

The time for your healing is now. Stop looking around at what others can't or won't do for you. Jesus, your healer, is right there in front of you. Listen to His voice and do what He tells you to do.

Three Steps to Claiming Your Healing:

1. *Speak up and say you want to be healed.*

2. *Look up. Other people can't heal you. Jesus can.*

3. *Push up. Do what Jesus tells you to do.*

THE TAKEAWAY: The wait is over and your time is now. Listen to the voice of Jesus, your healer.

WEDNESDAY - Delivered but Still Dabbling

THE TEXT: *"Afterward Jesus found him in the temple and said to him, 'See, you are well! Sin no more that nothing worse may happen to you'"* (John 5:14).

THE TALK: Jesus healed the man after He had been an invalid for thirty-eight years. But the man's healing was incomplete.

❄

He was healed of his infirmity, but his heart still needed work. Jesus found the man to let him know that he still had work to do. He needed to repent and reject his sin.

Sometimes we stop too soon. We experience deliverance, but we keep dabbling with what got us trapped in the first place. If we want a full life, we need to fill ourselves up with Jesus. Quit messing around with half-hearted obedience. Repent, reject your sin, and tell Jesus you want everything He has to give you.

Three Ways to Practice Whole-Hearted Obedience:

1. *Repent fully and stop flirting with sin.*

2. *Reject compromise and temptations.*

3. *Refuel your power by filling up on Jesus.*

THE TAKEAWAY: Repent, reject your sin, and get filled up on Jesus.

THURSDAY - Help My Unbelief!

THE TEXT: *"Immediately the father of the child cried out and said, 'I believe; help my unbelief!'" (Mark 9:24).*

THE TALK: When Jesus went up on the Mount of Transfiguration, He left most of His disciples down below. While Jesus was gone a father brought his demon-possessed son to the disciples, but the disciples were not able to cast it out. The father asked Jesus to cast the demon out of his son, saying "If you can." Jesus questioned the father's "if," reminding him that all things are possible for those who believe. Immediately the father cried out, "I believe, help my unbelief!"

The father confessed his inadequacy and his dependence on Jesus. He couldn't cast the demon out. He couldn't muster more than a tiny scrap of faith that Jesus could, but that small seed of faith and cry for help were all He needed. The faith Jesus was looking for was the man's willingness to admit his need. It's all we need, too. When you're stuck, looking for a breakthrough, and struggling to believe, cry out to Jesus. He answers when we admit our dependence on Him.

Three Things to Do When You're Struggling to Believe:

1. *Confess your doubt.*

2. *Admit your need.*

3. *Cry out to Jesus.*

THE TAKEAWAY: When you're struggling to believe, cry out to Jesus. He helps those who depend on Him.

FRIDAY - Making History

THE TEXT: *"And he said to them, 'This kind cannot be driven out by anything but prayer'" (Mark 9:29).*

THE TALK: The disciples didn't understand why Jesus could heal the demon-possessed boy but they could not. Perhaps they thought it was a matter of technique. In the first-century world, Jewish exorcists cast out demons through elaborate rituals and incantations. Jesus said it wasn't an issue of skill, but dependence. True spiritual power doesn't come from knowing the right words to say or techniques to try. True spiritual power flows from a relationship forged through our history with God. Prayer, Bible study, worship, and our history of obedience are the tools God uses to teach us who He is and who we are in relationship to Him. As we learn those lessons, our faith grows and we start to see what God can do. Victory begins on our knees.

Three Ways to Forge History with God:

1. *Spend time with God in prayer, worship, and Bible study.*

2. *Ask God to help you understand what He wants to do in your life.*

3. *When God opens a door, pray, believe, and walk on through.*

THE TAKEAWAY: If you want power from God, you need to live history with God.

WEEKEND REFLECTION

"Abide in me, and I in you. As the branch cannot bear fruit by itself, unless it abides in the vine, neither can you, unless you abide in me" (John 15:4).

FOR REFLECTION: Branches can't bear fruit unless they are connected to the vine. We can't bear fruit unless we are connected to Jesus. What are you doing to stay connected to Jesus? What spiritual disciplines help you abide in Him? How could you develop a rhythm of life that helps you stay connected to Jesus? Ask Jesus to increase your desire to abide in Him so your life bears abundant fruit.

_____

_____

_____

_____

_____

_____

_____

_____

Week Eleven

MONDAY - Tools of Transformation

THE TEXT: *"And they devoted themselves to the apostles' teaching and the fellowship, to the breaking of bread and to the prayers" (Acts 2:42).*

THE TALK: After the Holy Spirit came on the day of Pentecost, the first believers dedicated themselves to a few key practices. They devoted themselves to the study of Scripture through the apostles' teaching. They spent time in fellowship, building relationships with one another. They ate meals together in each other's homes. They prayed with power. And daily, God added to the number of those who were being saved.

If we want to see the Spirit's power at work, we should learn from the example of the early church. We can devote ourselves to the study of the Word. We can make space for relationships, opening our homes and eating meals together. And we can pray like we mean it. Word. Fellowship. Worship. Prayer. These are our tools of transformation.

Four Tools of Transformation:

1. *Spend time in God's Word.*

2. *Develop relationships with God's people.*

3. *Worship God's majesty and power.*

4. *Pray and ask God to show you His heart.*

THE TAKEAWAY: Pick up your tools of transformation and work with the Spirit's power.

❄

TUESDAY - Throwing Shade

THE TEXT: *"They even carried out the sick into the streets and laid them on cots and mats, that as Peter came by at least his shadow might fall on some of them" (Acts 5:15).*

THE TALK: Today when people talk about "throwing shade," they mean to trash talk someone, especially using sarcasm to make a point. Peter took that phrase in a whole different direction. The signs and wonders Peter and the other apostles were doing amazed people. They started bringing the sick out into the streets so that Peter's shadow would fall on them as he walked along. Many were healed—not because Peter was so powerful, but because God is.

Is there power in your shade? If we are filled with the Holy Spirit, we bring the Spirit's power with us when we walk in the room. We reflect the Son—Jesus. That kind of power can change the atmosphere. It can bring hope. It can bring transformation. It can point people to a better future. What kind of shade do you throw?

Three Ways to Put Power in Your Shade:

1. *Fill up with the Holy Spirit.*

2. *Desire to reflect the Son's glory.*

3. *Point people to God's power.*

THE TAKEAWAY: Your shade—your influence—should reflect the power of the Son.

WEDNESDAY - Treasure Hunters

THE TEXT: *"So Barnabas went to Tarsus to look for Saul, and when he had found him he brought him to Antioch" (Acts 11:25-26).*

THE TALK: Barnabas' name means "son of encouragement." Barnabas was the kind of person who saw potential in others. When the church began reaching large numbers of Gentiles for the first time, Barnabas needed help. Barnabas remembered Saul, the former persecutor of the church who had followed Christ after meeting Jesus on the Damascus Road. Barnabas went looking for him. The world hasn't been the same since.

We need more encouragers like Barnabas who see the potential in others. Too often we want people to get themselves cleaned up before we try to deal with them. But where we see a mess, encouragers see potential. They're willing to walk beside people, working out the kinks and showing them how to live. Those transformed lives can change the world.

Three Ways to Uncover Potential:

1. *Look for the best in people.*

2. *Ask God to reveal His destiny for those around you.*

3. *Bring them along with you as you experience what God is doing.*

THE TAKEAWAY: Don't be afraid of the mess. Be a Barnabas who sees potential in others.

THURSDAY - Reach Out and Touch Someone

THE TEXT: *"And God was doing extraordinary miracles by the hands of Paul, so that even handkerchiefs or aprons that had touched his skin were carried away to the sick, and their diseases left them and the evil spirits came out of them"* *(Acts 29:11-12).*

THE TALK: God displayed His power as Paul preached in Ephesus. God's anointing was so strong on Paul that whatever touched him carried His anointing. His touch brought healing and freedom.

What do you bring with your touch? You've heard it said that hurt people hurt people. Other things are contagious too. Happy people make people around them happy. Hospitable people make others feel at home. Kind people inspire kindness in others. How do you touch other people's lives?

Three Ways to Make Your Touch Count:

1. *Touch other people with kindness.*

2. *Touch other people with healing.*

3. *Touch other people with authentic power.*

THE TAKEAWAY: Use your touch to make the world around you better.

FRIDAY - Alternative Energy

THE TEXT: *"But the evil spirit answered them, 'Jesus I know and Paul I recognize, but who are you?'" (Acts 19:15).*

THE TALK: As Paul preached in Ephesus, others tried to imitate what he was doing. Jewish exorcists tried casting out evil spirits in the name of "Jesus who Paul proclaims." Seven sons of a Jewish priest named Sceva tried doing this, but the spirit didn't recognize their authority. The man with the evil spirit attacked them and overpowered them until all seven sons fled the house naked and wounded.

We can't borrow someone else's power. It can't come from our families, our friends, or any other alternative source. We can only get our power from Jesus. If you want power to deal with life's trouble and evil, you have to get it from the right place.

❅

Three Ways to Get Genuine Power:

1. *Reject any substitutes for God's power.*

2. *Refuse to lean on secondhand faith.*

3. *Receive God's power by plugging into Jesus.*

THE TAKEAWAY: Get your power by plugging into Jesus. No other source will do.

WEEKEND REFLECTION

"Now when they saw the boldness of Peter and John and perceived that they were uneducated, common men, they were astonished. And they recognized that they had been with Jesus" (Acts 4:13).

FOR REFLECTION: When the Jewish leaders heard Peter and John speak, they were astonished that men with no formal rabbinical training could speak with such power and boldness. However, they recognized that they had been with Jesus. When people look at your life, can they tell you have been with Jesus? What is one thing you have done this week to spend time with Jesus? What is one thing you could do in the week to come? Ask God to help you live in a way that shows others you have been with Jesus.

Week Twelve

MONDAY - Inherit Your Destiny

THE TEXT: *"Now the Lord said to Abram, 'Go from your country and your kindred and your father's house to the land that I will show you'" (Genesis 12:1).*

THE TALK: God had a destiny for Abram. But Abram couldn't stay where he was to receive it. To receive his destiny, Abram had to embrace change.

We must also embrace change to inherit the destiny God has for us. God told Abram he had a future, but Abram had to act in faith by going to the place God had for him. In the same way, we need to let God show us our destiny and move toward it. Moving into our destiny stretches us. It forces us to leave the places where we feel comfortable and safe to embrace the unfamiliar and the unknown. But there is no place we can go where God isn't already there. Go after your destiny.

Three Ways to Embrace Change:

1. *Learn to find comfort in God's closeness instead of your circumstances.*

2. *Give up control and put God in charge.*

3. *Remember there's no place you can go where God isn't already there.*

THE TAKEAWAY: Make the changes you need to make to go after your destiny.

TUESDAY - Distracting Detours

THE TEXT: *"Now there was a famine in the land. So Abram went down to Egypt to sojourn there, for the famine was severe in the land" (Genesis 12:10).*

THE TALK: When famine struck the land of Canaan, Abram took his family and headed down to Egypt. It wasn't Abram's finest moment. Abram's wife, Sarai, was beautiful, and Abram was afraid the Egyptians would kill him to take her. He told Sarai to lie and say that Abram was her brother and not her husband. He kept up the pretense even after Pharaoh claimed Sarai for himself. God himself had to intervene to rescue Sarai.

We may also face detours on the way to our destiny, but when difficulties arise, we need to continue to seek God's direction. Don't look for shortcuts or use deception or manipulation to get your way. God is the one leading you to your destiny. When you face detours, get your directions from Him.

Three Ways to Avoid Detours:

1. When difficulties come, seek God's direction.

2. Refuse to take shortcuts on the way to your destiny.

3. Wait for God's solution, then follow Him.

THE TAKEAWAY: Let God direct you on the way to your destiny.

WEDNESDAY - If None Go with Me

THE TEXT: *"Abram settled in the land of Canaan, while Lot settled among the cities of the valley and moved his tent as far as Sodom" (Genesis 13:12).*

THE TALK: Abram's nephew Lot accompanied him on the journey to Canaan. Both Abram and Lot grew wealthy in Canaan, and their flocks multiplied until the land couldn't support them both. Abram realized they would have to separate. He graciously let Lot choose which portion of the land he wanted. Lot headed east, away from Abram and toward the sinful city of Sodom. It was the beginning of his fall.

Not everyone is going to accompany you on the way to your destiny. Friends may not understand your purpose. Family members may wonder who you think you are. Some people will start out the journey with you but take a different path along the way. Let them. Your job is to be obedient to what God has called you to do. Moving toward your destiny may mean moving away from people who don't believe the promise God has given you.

When Destiny Leads You in A Different Direction:

1. *Accept that not everyone will go with you on the way to your destiny.*

2. *Resolutely move toward God's promise.*

3. *Look for people who will chase your destiny with you.*

THE TAKEAWAY: Not everyone will follow you to your destiny. Look for the people who will chase your destiny with you.

THURSDAY – Dry Holes and Empty Wells

THE TEXT: *"But Abram said to the king of Sodom, 'I have lifted my hand to the Lord...that I would not take a thread or a sandal strap or anything that is yours'"* (Genesis 13:21-22).

THE TALK: War broke out between the kings of Sodom and Gomorrah and the kings of some of the surrounding peoples. The enemy ransacked Sodom and Gomorrah and took the people captive, including Lot, Abram's nephew. Abram defeated the enemy and rescued Lot and the other captives. The king of Sodom offered to let Abram keep the plunder for himself, but Abram refused. He would not let the king of Sodom say he was the one to make Abram rich.

We can't accept substitutes on the way to our destiny. The wealth of Sodom may have looked good, but it was only a dry hole. No human king could deliver the destiny God had promised Abram, and no human source can deliver the destiny God has promised us. Reject substitutes and shortcuts that only leave you thirsting. The destiny God has for you will truly satisfy.

Three Ways to Recognize Substitutes and Shortcuts:

1. *Substitutes and shortcuts look good but leave you thirsty.*

2. *Substitutes and shortcuts try to take God's place and steal God's glory.*

3. *Substitutes and shortcuts pale in comparison to the reality of God's promise.*

THE TAKEAWAY: Reject the substitutes and shortcuts that can distract you from your destiny.

FRIDAY - Living the Dream

THE TEXT: *"And [the Lord] brought him outside and said, 'Look toward heaven, and number the stars if you are able to number them.' Then he said to him, 'So shall your offspring be'"* (Genesis 15:5).

THE TALK: Abram's name meant "exalted father," but he was a childless man with a barren wife. Though it seemed impossible, God promised Abram's descendants would be as numerous as the stars in the sky. God's promise went far beyond anything Abram had imagined or dreamed, and God kept His promise. We who follow Christ also follow in Abram's footsteps of faith. We are the offspring God promised.

We will miss out if we don't let God determine our destiny. God's plans for us are beyond anything we could imagine or dream. Don't settle for what you think is possible or achievable. Let God lead you into the God-sized dream He has for you.

Three Ways to Embrace God's Promise:

1. *Don't settle for what you think you can do.*

2. *Dream big and ask what God wants to do through you.*

3. *Cultivate a desire for the destiny God wants to give you.*

THE TAKEAWAY: Don't settle for what you can do. Let God show you the destiny He wants to create for you.

WEEKEND REFLECTION

"And [Abram] believed the Lord, and he counted it to him as righteousness" (Genesis 15:6).

FOR REFLECTION: Abram believed God's promise, and on the basis of his faith, God considered Abram to be in a right relationship with Himself. When we believe Christ's promise, God credits us with righteousness. How are you doing at believing what God has promised? What tempts you to give way to doubt? What encourages you to hold firm in faith? Ask God to increase your faith as you move toward your destiny.

❄

Week Thirteen

MONDAY - Name Recognition

THE TEXT: *"A good name is to be chosen rather than great riches, and favor is better than silver or gold" (Proverbs 22:1).*

THE TALK: The theme song for the TV show *Cheers* talked about how great it is for everyone to know your name. We like being known. It feels good to be recognized, appreciated, and accepted. We can choose and develop our own names because of what Christ has done for us. Some of us have family legacies of faith. Some don't. Either way, we can claim the name of our Heavenly Father. Choose to live like a man or woman who carries Christ's name. Develop your name by leaving a legacy of spiritual fruit: love, joy, peace, patience, kindness, goodness, gentleness, faithfulness, and self-control. Live in such a way that people can recognize you as a child of God.

How to Develop Name Recognition:

1. *Develop your name by leaving a fruitful legacy.*

2. *Claim the name of your Heavenly Father.*

3. *Introduce yourself with the name God has given you: His.*

THE TAKEAWAY: Tell people your real name: Child of God.

TUESDAY - Undefeated

THE TEXT: *"Now to him who is able to keep you from stumbling and to present you blameless before the presence of his glory with great joy" (Jude 24).*

THE TALK: If you've ever played sports, you know how hard it is to have an undefeated season. One mistake, one bad night, or one key player out with an injury can lead to a loss for even the best team. But God has the power to bring us through undefeated. Christ is able to keep us from stumbling and present us to himself blameless. He takes joy in our victory. But you can't be undefeated if you never get in the game. Don't restrict yourself to the sidelines because you're afraid of failure and defeat. Get in the game and play. You will win because you are more than a conqueror. Jesus has already won the victory and He will present you blameless.

Winning the Game:

1. *You are undefeated and blameless because of what God has done.*

2. *You will win because of Christ.*

3. *You have to get up and play to share the victory.*

THE TAKEAWAY: Christ is calling your number. Get in the game and share in the victory.

WEDNESDAY - Are You Full of It?

THE TEXT: *"He must increase, but I must decrease"* (John 3:30).

THE TALK: It's important to check the fluids in your car to keep it running properly. Your oil, transmission fluid, radiator fluid, and brake fluid all help keep your engine working well. When your fluids get low, you need to top them off. To keep our spiritual engines running well, we must be filled up on Jesus. But to fill up on Jesus, we have to get ourselves out of the way. When we're consumed with chasing what we want, what pleases us, and what we think makes us look good, our lives get so filled to the capacity with self that there's no room for anything else. We have to decrease so Jesus can increase—living in a way that makes people talk about how great Jesus is and not how great we are. Fill up on Jesus, and don't stop till you get all of Him you need.

Get Your Fill:

1. *Check your levels. Are you full of you or full of Jesus?*

2. *Pour out through service so you always have room to fill up with more of Jesus.*

3. *Keep getting filled. Don't stop till you get enough of Jesus.*

THE TAKEAWAY: Check your levels. What's filling your tank? Fill up on Jesus.

THURSDAY - He's in You

THE TEXT: *"He who is in you is greater than he who is in the world" (1 John 4:4).*

THE TALK: What obstacles or challenges are in your life? When the going gets tough, one simple truth can help you overcome: God is in you.

The power of God in you is greater than the forces and powers of this world. God's power is in you, and that makes you stronger than you think. If you feel weak, it's okay. It's not your strength that matters—it's His. The problem may be big, but you are stronger than the problem. Maybe the past has left you feeling beat up and smashed down, but you are stronger than yesterday. The power of God in you will help you overcome.

Three Truths to Remember:

1. *You are stronger than you think.*

2. *You are stronger than the problem.*

3. *You are stronger than yesterday.*

THE TAKEAWAY: The same God who created the universe is living in you. How can you be defeated?

FRIDAY - Running Unopposed

THE TEXT: *"If God is for us, who can be against us?"* (Romans 8:31).

THE TALK: Maybe you're facing opposition in your life. People think this Jesus thing you've got going is a little strange. They don't understand why you won't do the things they do. Maybe they accuse you of trying to puff yourself up or acting holier-than-thou. Maybe they even try to put you in your place or knock you down. But what does it matter? God is for you. They can't stop you or get in your way. Don't waste time on fighting your opposition. Put your focus on pleasing Him.

Three Ways to Face Your Opposition:

1. *Remember that God is for you. Your opposition doesn't matter.*

2. *Don't waste time on fighting your opposition. They're already defeated.*

3. *Put your focus on pleasing God. Your victory comes from Him.*

THE TAKEAWAY: Don't worry about your opposition. God is for you. Who can be against you?

WEEKEND REFLECTION

"For by you I can run against a troop, and by my God I can leap over a wall" (Psalm 18:29).

FOR REFLECTION: David wrote the words of this Psalm after God delivered him from King Saul. He knew that God gave him the strength to defeat any enemy and conquer any obstacle. What obstacles are you facing? What is keeping you from chasing the destiny and purpose God has for you? What holds you back from fulfilling God's calling on your life? Ask God to give you the strength to overcome.

_____

_____

_____

_____

_____

_____

_____

_____

_____

_____

_____

_____

_____

_____

❄

DEVOTIONS FOR

Spring

Week Fourteen

MONDAY - Wait for What?

THE TEXT: *"Wait for the Lord; be strong, and let your heart take courage; wait for the Lord!" (Psalm 27:14).*

THE TALK: Do you ever feel like you've run out of patience? Sometimes as we wait we may wonder if God knows what time it is. But He does. God knows the *kronos* time—chronological time, or the time on your wristwatch. God knows the *kairos* time—the divine time, or the opportune time for things to happen. And God knows the *teleos* time—the time for purposes to be completed or fulfilled. If we are waiting, we can trust God's timing is always right. Our waiting shouldn't be filled with wonder and worry. Our waiting time is a season of preparation and expectancy. Fill your waiting time with worship.

Waiting Well:

1. *Remember, God knows the time.*

2. *Use your wait time to get ready for your divine appointment.*

3. *Fill your waiting time with worship.*

THE TAKEAWAY: Don't worry while you wait. Use your waiting time to worship.

TUESDAY - It Had to Die

THE TEXT: *"Then Jesus told them plainly, 'Lazarus has died'"* (John 11:14).

THE TALK: When Jesus heard that Lazarus was sick, His disciples expected Him to leave right away. But Jesus waited two more days. By the time Jesus left, Lazarus was already dead. But death isn't the end when Jesus is around. Sometimes things have to die before you can get to the resurrection. Trying to hang on and pump life into something that is meant to die may just be delaying your miracle. It's hard to let go, but new life is waiting on the other side. It has to die for you see the resurrection.

Let it Die:

1. *Let it die because Jesus isn't coming until it does.*

2. *Let it die because part of you needs to die, too.*

3. *Let it die because God's glory will rise.*

THE TAKEAWAY: Let it die. Death leads to resurrection.

WEDNESDAY - Take the Grave Clothes Off

THE TEXT: *"The man who had died came out, his hands and feet bound with linen strips, and his face wrapped with a cloth. Jesus said to them, 'Unbind him, and let him go'"* (John 11:44).

THE TALK: Lazarus had been in the tomb for four days. Everyone thought it was over. But then Jesus showed up. Jesus raised Lazarus from the grave, and he came out of the tomb still wrapped in the grave clothes.

It's not over till Jesus shows up. Jesus is the resurrection and the life—the living embodiment of God's resurrection power. And His power is alive and well and working in you. You are a witness to the power of our Almighty God. What looks like death doesn't have to be the end. Get those grave clothes off, and let Jesus bring forth new life in you.

Death isn't the End:

1. *It's not over till Jesus shows up.*

2. *Get some help to get the grave clothes off.*

3. *Testify about Jesus' resurrection power.*

THE TAKEAWAY: It's not over till Jesus shows up. Testify to His resurrection power.

THURSDAY - The After Party

THE TEXT: *"Many of the Jews therefore, who had come with Mary and had seen what he did, believed in him, but some of them went to the Pharisees and told them what Jesus had done"* (John 11:45-46).

THE TALK: Lazarus had been dead for four days when Jesus raised him from the dead. It was a definitive declaration of Jesus' resurrection power, and people celebrated. When God blesses you, be ready for the after party. People are going to want to rejoice with you.

But while some will receive your blessing, others will reject it. Some people saw Lazarus' rise as a threat, and they went running to the Pharisees to tattletale on Jesus. Some people will see your rise as a threat, too. Don't let them rain on your parade. Keep talking about what God has done and what He's going to do. And don't get too haughty, either. Stay humble and give God the glory as you enjoy the party. Not everyone is going to come to your party. Celebrate anyway.

When People Don't Come to Your Party:

1. *Recognize that not everyone is going to celebrate with you.*

2. *Keep talking about what God has done and what God is going to do.*

3. *Don't get proud. Give God the glory for blessing you.*

THE TAKEAWAY: Don't invite everyone to the after party of your blessings. Celebrate with those who will praise God with you.

FRIDAY - Prayerful Pause

THE TEXT: *"I cried aloud to the Lord, and he answered me from his holy hill. Selah" (Psalm 3:4).*

THE TALK: The word *selah* occurs at least seventy-four times in the Bible. *Selah* is a Hebrew musical term that probably means something along the lines of "silence" or "pause." Some think it indicates a moment of reflection after an emotional experience or invocation.

We need *selah* pauses in our life. We need *selah* after victory as we pause to reflect on the meaning of the moment and how we got this far. We need *selah* after defeat as we mourn our loss and figure out how to pick up the pieces. And we need *selah* in the midst of battle, pausing to cry out to the Lord who always hears and responds to our cry. When emotions are high, *selah* moments reorient us to God and remind us of who He is.

Take a Selah Moment:

1. *After victory.*

2. *After defeat.*

3. *In the midst of battle.*

THE TAKEAWAY: Be on the lookout for your next *selah* moment. When it comes, cry out to God and He will answer you.

WEEKEND REFLECTION

"My soul waits for the Lord more than watchmen for the morning" (Psalm 130:6).

FOR REFLECTION: Watchmen know the morning is going to come. The night may be long, dark, dangerous, and cold, but sooner or later dawn will break over the horizon. Morning is sure, and God's coming is as certain as the morning. What are you waiting for this week? Don't lose hope. The night may feel long, but God will come to you as surely as the dawn. Ask God to help you wait expectantly for His coming.

Week Fifteen

MONDAY - Leave it Better

THE TEXT: *"But seek the welfare of the city where I have sent you into exile, and pray to the Lord on its behalf, for in its welfare you will find your welfare"* (Jeremiah 29:7).

THE TALK: Jeremiah's message to the people wasn't what they wanted to hear. The Jews in exile in Babylon wanted to go home. But through His prophet, God told the people to make their homes in Babylon and work for the good of the city. As the city prospered, so would they.

As the people of God, we also have a responsibility to work for the good of the communities where God has placed us. We are to pray for our cities, look for opportunities to bless those around us, and make our communities better. So, pray for your city. Take your neighbors supper or offer to mow their yard. Build a park. Paint over graffiti. Pick up trash. Volunteer. God blesses us as we bless our communities.

Three Ways to Bless Your Community:

1. *Pay attention to needs. How can you help meet them?*

2. *Get involved. Speak up. Show Up. Volunteer.*

3. *Be relational. Treat people like treasure. Value them.*

THE TAKEAWAY: Pray for your community, bless it, and make it better.

TUESDAY - Breaking Through

THE TEXT: *"As soon as I heard these words I sat down and wept and mourned for days, and I continued fasting and praying before the God of heaven" (Nehemiah 1:4).*

THE TALK: Never underestimate the power of prayer and fasting. Nehemiah grieved when he heard that Jerusalem was in distress. Broken walls left the city defenseless. Nehemiah responded to the news with prayer and fasting, and God brought breakthrough. God gave Nehemiah the opportunity to tell the king about Jerusalem, and the king commissioned Nehemiah to return home and rebuild Jerusalem's wall. If you want to see breakthrough, build your prayer life. Develop the habit of corporate prayer. Enlist intercessors. Dedicate yourself to prayer and fasting. Breakthroughs come through prayer.

How to Achieve Breakthrough:

1. *Pray sincerely.*

2. *Pray corporately.*

3. *Pray continually.*

THE TAKEAWAY: Devote yourself to prayer to bring the breakthrough.

WEDNESDAY - Someone Else Can Do It

THE TEXT: *"You and the people with you will certainly wear yourselves out, for the thing is too heavy for you. You are not able to do it alone" (Exodus 18:18).*

THE TALK: After Moses led the Hebrew people out of Egypt, his father-in-law Jethro came to see him. Jethro gave Moses some needed advice. When the people had conflicts, they brought them to Moses to judge. Moses heard them all himself, but it was wearing him out. Jethro realized Moses needed to delegate. Jethro told Moses to appoint trustworthy people who could judge minor matters and bring the important cases to him. Delegating would free Moses to do what he really needed to do: listen to the Lord and lead the people.

Sometimes if we want it done right, we have to get someone else to do it. We shouldn't cheat others out of their chance to serve. Delegating frees us to focus on our callings and allows others the chance to develop theirs. Share success by letting others shine.

Three Reasons to Delegate:

1. *It allows others a chance to serve.*

2. *It frees us to focus on our callings.*

3. *It develops leaders for the future.*

THE TAKEAWAY: Sharing responsibilities with others allows them to fulfill their callings as you fulfill yours.

THURSDAY - Equally Gifted

THE TEXT: *"For just as the body is one and has many members, and all the members of the body, though many, are one body, so it is with Christ"* (1 Corinthians 12:12).

THE TALK: It would be ridiculous for a hand to think it's not important because it isn't an eye, or for an eye to think it isn't important because it isn't the heart. All the parts of our body are important and work together so the body functions properly. And so it is with the church. We can't think we aren't important because we clean up after fellowship meals instead of teaching Sunday School or believe serving in the nursery is least important than serving in the choir. All our gifts are important and all our gifts matter. We need to use our gifts for God's glory and for the benefit of God's people.

Three Truths about Spiritual Gifts:

1. *All gifts are given by God.*

2. *All gifts matter.*

3. *All gifts are meant to be used. Find a place to serve.*

THE TAKEAWAY: Your gift matters to the body of Christ. Use it well.

FRIDAY - Privilege and Responsibility

THE TEXT: *"And he gave the apostles, the prophets, the evangelists, the shepherds and teachers, to equip the saints for the work of ministry, for the building up of the body of Christ" (Ephesians 4:11-12).*

THE TALK: It's not the preacher's job to do the work of the church. It doesn't matter how big your church is or how many ministers you have on staff. The ministry of the church is not their job. It's yours. God has placed leaders in the church to equip the saints to do the work of the ministry—not to do it all themselves. You have the privilege and responsibility of helping your church carry out its task of proclaiming the gospel and reaching your world. Don't be a pew filler. Be a ministry partner, carrying Christ's message to the world.

Do the Work:

1. *The privilege and responsibility of ministry is your job.*

2. *Be a ministry partner, not a pew sitter.*

3. *Find a way you can help take the gospel to the world.*

THE TAKEAWAY: All followers of Christ should be involved in ministry. Find your place and get to work.

WEEKEND REFLECTION

"But as it is, God arranged the members in the body, each one of them, as he chose" (1 Corinthians 12:18).

FOR REFLECTION: God has placed us in the body of Christ as He chose. You are not in your church on accident. Neither are the people you worship with on Sunday morning. God has chosen to put you there to love, serve, and learn from one another. How are you fulfilling your role as a part of the body? How are you serving and showing love? Who are you teaching? Who are you learning from? Ask God to show you how you can bring glory to Him as an active part of your local church.

_____

_____

_____

_____

_____

_____

_____

_____

_____

_____

_____

_____

Week Sixteen

MONDAY – One in a Billion

THE TEXT: *"You know when I sit down and when I rise up; you discern my thoughts from afar"* (Psalm 139:2).

THE TALK: You are one in a billion. God made you on purpose, and no one can take your place. Remember how in school when you had a substitute teacher, nothing felt quite the same when you stepped into the classroom? You needed your regular teacher to be present for real learning to take place. In the same way, God made you absolutely unique. No one else can fill your shoes or do the work God has ordained you to do. God knows you perfectly and has perfectly created you to play a part in His kingdom designed for you. Be yourself. No one else will do.

Being You:

1. *God made you on purpose.*

2. *There's a place in God's kingdom designed for you.*

3. *Don't send in a substitute. There's only one you.*

THE TAKEAWAY: Just be you. There are no substitutes for you.

TUESDAY – How Strong are You?

THE TEXT: *"Finally, be strong in the Lord and in the strength of his might"* (Ephesians 6:10).

THE TALK: At the gym, sometimes people use a spotter to help them lift weights. For certain exercises like doing a bench press, the spotter helps ensure the lifter's safety. A spotter helps you lift or push more weight than you could normally lift safely. Good spotters watch your form and know when to step in and help you carry the weight.

Sometimes we don't know how strong we are until we get to something we can't lift. That's when we have to rely on God's strength, not our own. When you're looking at a weight you think you can't carry, don't be afraid. Jesus will spot you. He lends you His strength when you need help to carry the load. That weight isn't going to kill you. It will make you stronger.

How Strong Are You?

1. *You don't know your strength until you get to a weight you can't lift.*

2. *Jesus will spot you.*

3. *The weight won't kill you. It will make you stronger.*

THE TAKEAWAY: Jesus is your spotter when the load is heavy. His strength makes you stronger.

WEDNESDAY - Can You Handle the Truth?

THE TEXT: *"But Jesus on his part did not entrust himself to them"* (John 2:24).

THE TALK: When Jesus began His ministry, many people were drawn to the miracles He was doing. But Jesus did not entrust himself to them. They weren't ready. They didn't believe who He was or understand why He had come, and they weren't willing to hear Him and receive His message. They lacked the capacity to handle Jesus.

Can you handle the truth about Jesus? What a tragedy it must be to have Jesus right there in front of you and not be willing to embrace all that He wants to give you. But how often do we do the same thing, trying to force Jesus to do what we want instead of trying to understand who He wants us to be? Do you have the faith to believe Jesus is who He says He is? Does your character demonstrate He can trust you to do what He wants you to do? And will you honor Jesus or attempt to use Him for your own ends? How much Jesus can you be trusted with?

Three Things that Determine How Much Jesus You Can Handle:

1. *The strength of your faith.*

2. *The quality of your character.*

3. *The purity of your motives.*

THE TAKEAWAY: Do a self-check and determine your capacity for Jesus.

THURSDAY - Guard Your Lips

THE TEXT: *"Set a guard, O Lord, over my mouth; keep watch over the door of my lips!" (Psalm 141:3).*

THE TALK: Our words have power. Words can build up or tear down, create or destroy. Our words can inspire love, beauty, and honor, but they can also inspire bigotry, hatred, and violence. We need to learn to use our words well. Our words reflect who we are and what we do. Our minds, hearts, thoughts, and desires are all connected to what comes out of our mouths. But words also create our worlds. Our words are what we use to describe the reality made up of our values, beliefs, and experiences. Over time our words both define and create that reality. Be careful of what you say. That may be what you become.

Three Ways to Guard Your Lips:

1. *Speak truth. Speak what God says is true.*

2. *Speak life. Speak blessing, not destruction.*

3. *Speak faith. Speak of who God is and what He has promised to do.*

THE TAKEAWAY: Your words have power. Use them well.

FRIDAY - Pray Without Ceasing

THE TEXT: *"Pray without ceasing" (1 Thessalonians 5:17).*

THE TALK: There are two words you hate to hear from your doctor: *lifestyle change.* It means you can't just take a pill to get better. You're going to have to do some work for the long haul—eating healthy and exercising until it stops being a diet and becomes the way you live. Praying without ceasing is a prescription for lifestyle change. It means living a lifestyle of prayer so that prayer becomes your first response and not your last resort. Pray when you're happy and when you're sad. Pray when you win and win you lose. Pray when you wake up, when you leave the house, and when you turn your lamp out at night. Pray about everything and every situation everywhere. Develop a lifestyle of continual prayer.

Developing a Lifestyle of Prayer:

1. *Pray with two-way communication: listen and talk.*

2. *Use simple words to call out to the Father.*

3. *Pray relationally. Pray for others as well as for yourself.*

THE TAKEAWAY: Develop a lifestyle of prayer so prayer is your first response, not your last resort.

WEEKEND REFLECTION

"Let each one of you speak the truth with his neighbor, for we are members of one another" (Ephesians 4:25).

FOR REFLECTION: As followers of Christ, we are meant to be people who speak the truth. How can anyone trust that the gospel is true if we are known as people who practice deceit? How have you done at speaking the truth this week? In what areas could you improve at speaking truth? Ask God to give you the courage to be a truth teller.

_____

_____

_____

_____

_____

_____

_____

_____

_____

_____

_____

_____

Week Seventeen

MONDAY - State of Mind

THE TEXT: *"In any and every circumstance, I have learned the secret of facing plenty and hunger, abundance and need. I can do all things through him who strengthens me"* *(Philippians 4:12-13).*

THE TALK: Contentment is not dependent on our conditions. Too often we think contentment is found in having a little more than what we have now. A slightly bigger house. A few more dollars in the bank account. A couple more days off work. A newer version of our phone or tablet. But contentment is not a matter of what you have. Contentment is a matter of who has you. Paul found contentment in times of plenty and times of hunger, in times of abundance and in times of need. As he sat in a Roman jail cell, he was able to write about the secret of contentment because the source of his contentment was Jesus. What mattered wasn't his condition, but the conditioning of his mind. It was fixed on Jesus. And it's the same with us. We won't find contentment by going after more stuff. We find contentment by going after more of Jesus.

Three Characteristics of Contentment:

1. *Contentment isn't a matter of what you have but whether Jesus has you.*

2. *Contentment depends on the conditioning of your mind, not your physical condition.*

3. *The secret of contentment is being content with Jesus.*

THE TAKEAWAY: Find contentment by going after more of Jesus.

TUESDAY - Know Your Limits

THE TEXT: *"I can do all things through him who strengthens me" (Philippians 4:13).*

THE TALK: Speed limits are there for our safety. Wide-open stretches of freeway may let you speed along at seventy-five miles an hour, but twisty mountain roads, quiet neighborhoods, and school zones require you to slow down for your safety and for the safety of others. Living within limits requires us to adapt our speed to the conditions. Paul discovered his spiritual speed limit by following Jesus. He let Jesus dictate his speed—showing him when it was safe to speed up and when he needed to slow down. And as he did so, he found he could do more than he could have ever dreamed by living at the speed of Christ. Whose speed limits are you following?

Check Your Speed:

1. *Who's setting your limits—you or Jesus?*

2. *Don't be guilty of a DOJ—Driving Without Jesus.*

3. *Watch Jesus for your cues and learn to travel at His speed.*

THE TAKEAWAY: Learn to live at the speed of Christ.

WEDNESDAY - Enough to Go Around

THE TEXT: *"John was also baptizing at Aenon near Salim, because water was plentiful there, and people were coming and being baptized" (John 3:23).*

THE TALK: John came to prepare the way for Jesus' coming, but there was a brief period of time during which their ministries overlapped. After Jesus was baptized and before John was arrested, Jesus was preaching and baptizing in the Judean countryside. John was preaching and baptizing, too. Some of John's disciples complained, but John told them there was no competition. John's mission was to point people to Jesus. He was ending his mission as Jesus began His, and there was water enough for everyone. Other people's success doesn't threaten yours. There's room in God's kingdom for everyone.

How to Share the Water:

1. *Stop worrying about who's in the water with you. There's enough work for everyone.*

2. *Stop worrying about if there's enough water to go around. There's enough room for everyone.*

3. *Remember that you aren't competing, and let your promotion come from God.*

THE TAKEAWAY: In God's kingdom we are colleagues, not competitors. There's enough work for everyone.

THURSDAY - No Competition

THE TEXT: *"Outdo one another in showing honor"* (Romans 12:10).

THE TALK: Scarcity is one of the factors that drives prices. When commodities are plentiful, prices go down. When they are scarce, prices go up. Companies try to get consumers to perceive that items are scarce so customers will be willing to pay more for those products. But in the body of Christ, there is no scarcity of honor. We don't have to worry that we will run out. We can honor veterans and still honor nursery workers. We can honor the homeless and honor our first responders. We can honor the pastors, the worship team, Bible study leaders, and the folks who clean the bathrooms when we're all gone. There is enough honor to go around. And the only way we're to compete is not by gaining honor for ourselves, but in showing honor for others.

Three Ways to Show Honor:

1. *Learn to see people who serve you—baristas, checkers, janitors—and treat them like people.*

2. *Give other people credit for a job well done.*

3. *Publicly and prominently thank those who serve.*

THE TAKEAWAY: Compete to give honor, not to gain it.

FRIDAY - Just Follow Orders

THE TEXT: *"His mother said to the servants, 'Do whatever he tells you'"* (John 2:5).

THE TALK: Jesus performed His first miracle at a wedding. Early in Jesus' ministry, He was invited to a wedding. He went, along with His disciples. Then the wine ran out. That may not seem like a big problem to us, but for the bride and groom it was a major embarrassment. Mary, Jesus' mother, asked Jesus to do something. At first Jesus demurred, saying it wasn't yet His time. But Mary just turned to the servants and told them to follow Jesus' commands. He told the servants to take several ceremonial stone jars that were standing nearby, fill them with water, and take some to the master of the feast. When they did, they discovered that the water had turned to wine. When you follow Jesus' commands, miracles happen.

How to Follow Jesus' Commands:

1. *Don't question, just do. Servants follow commands.*

2. *Let what comes come. Miracles happen in the doing.*

3. *Remember that Jesus always gives the best.*

THE TAKEAWAY: Follow Jesus' orders today.

WEEKEND REFLECTION

"But he said, 'Blessed rather are those who hear the word of God and keep it!'" (Luke 11:28).

FOR REFLECTION: There is blessing in following God's commands. It's not just a matter of hearing God's Word—obedience requires us to hear God's commands and put them into practice. What are some of the blessings of obedience? How have you experienced these blessings? Ask God to help you hear and keep His Word.

_____

_____

_____

_____

_____

_____

_____

_____

_____

_____

_____

_____

_____

_____

Week Eighteen

MONDAY - It's Not the Cause—It's the Cure!

THE TEXT: *"Jesus answered, 'It was not that this man sinned, or his parents, but that the works of God might be displayed in him'"* (John 9:3).

THE TALK: One day Jesus and His disciples saw a man who had been blind from birth. In biblical times, people thought that illnesses and disabilities resulted from either the person's sin or sin somewhere in the family tree. When the disciples saw the blind man, they wanted to know whose fault it was. Was he blind because he had sinned or because his parents had?

The disciples were missing the point. The disciples saw a problem. They forgot Jesus was the cure. The man wasn't blind because of his sin or his parents' sin. His blindness was an opportunity for God to display His glory. Jesus healed the man.

Like the disciples, sometimes we focus too much on our own problems, trying to find the cause instead of looking for the cure. Jesus is the cure. Your condition is an opportunity for God to show His glory. Fix your eyes on Jesus and look for what God wants to do in you.

Three Steps to Fix Your Focus:

1. Stop focusing on the problem.

2. Wash your eyes out by focusing on Jesus.

3. Let God display His glory in you.

THE TAKEAWAY: Stop focusing on your condition and look for the cure. God wants to display His glory in you.

TUESDAY - God's Got This

THE TEXT: *"Be careful, be quiet, do not fear, and do not let your heart be faint because of these two smoldering stumps of firebrands" (Isaiah 7:4).*

THE TALK: Ahaz, the king of Judah, was terrified. The kings of Syria and Israel wanted Ahaz to join them in a coalition against Assyria. When Ahaz refused, Syria and Israel went to war against Judah to overthrow Ahaz and put a king on the throne who would be sympathetic to their plans. But God sent the prophet Isaiah to tell Ahaz not to fear. Israel and Syria posed no threat. In a short time, their nations would be overthrown. They were only the stumps of burned out firebrands—two leftover pieces of coal that posed no threat.

Sometimes life leaves us shaking in our shoes, but often what we think is a looming catastrophe is only a piece of coal left over from a previous battle. God's got you. Don't be afraid.

When Fear Leaves You Shaking:

1. *Remember that God knows about and cares about your problem.*

2. *Believe that no weapon formed against you will prosper.*

3. *Look for the smoke. The smoldering means the fire is over without you ever putting it out.*

THE TAKEAWAY: God began dealing with your problem before you knew you had one. He's got you.

WEDNESDAY - The Voice

THE TEXT: *"He said, 'I am the voice of one crying out in the wilderness, 'Make straight the name of the Lord' as the prophet Isaiah said'" (John 1:23).*

THE TALK: People didn't know what to think when John showed up on the scene. His camel hair robe looked strange. His diet of locusts and honey was unappealing, and he spoke like a prophet. Israel hadn't seen one of those for four hundred years. Some though he was Elijah back from the dead. Some thought he was Moses returned to give them a new law. Some thought he was the Messiah himself. But John insisted he was none of these. He was the forerunner, sent to prepare the people for Jesus to come.

We also have the job of getting people ready for Jesus' coming. We are the advance team, getting everything prepared for the Lord's appearance. We do that by telling people he is coming. We proclaim the gospel, and we coach them in how to respond. Today, people still get ready for Jesus in the same way they did in John's time: repenting from their sins and turning to follow Jesus.

How to Prepare the Way:

1. *Prepare your own heart. Are you ready?*

2. *Speak up. Proclaim the good news about Jesus.*

3. *Point people to Jesus.*

THE TAKEAWAY: Join the advance team and help get people ready for Jesus to come.

THURSDAY - Looking for the Sick

THE TEXT: *"Those who are well have no need of a physician, but those who are sick. I came not to call the righteous, but sinners"* (Mark 2:17).

THE TALK: Jesus sought out those who society had marginalized. His focus wasn't on society's best and brightest. He didn't court the favor of the religious leaders or political officials who held worldly power. Jesus knew sick people need a doctor, and that's who He went looking for. He was looking for people living on the margins of life.

Maybe that describes you. Maybe you've got a physical problem that has isolated you. Maybe you're struggling with depression or some other form of mental illness that society doesn't understand. Or maybe you've been knocked down too many times. Regardless, now you're wondering why Jesus would want to waste His time with you. But Jesus-time is never wasted time. He came for the sick to heal them, for the broken to make them whole, and for sinners to make them righteous. Reach out to Him. He's looking for you.

Jesus Looks for:

1. *People who are broken and want to be made whole.*

2. *People on the outside who want to come in.*

3. *People who are sinners and who want to be made right with God.*

THE TAKEAWAY: If you're sick, broken, or sinful, reach out. Jesus is looking for you.

FRIDAY - Cut the Drama

THE TEXT: *"Prompted by her mother, she said, 'Give me the head of John the Baptist here on a platter" (Matthew 14:8).*

THE TALK: Herod threw John the Baptist in prison because John had publicly called out his sin. He wanted to put John to death, but he hesitated because he feared what the people might do. On his birthday, his wife's daughter danced before him. Herod was so pleased with her performance that he promised to give her whatever she asked for. At her mother's prompting, the girl asked for John the Baptist's head on the platter. The public request forced Herod's hand, and he had John executed.

There is always going to be drama when you make decisions in the flesh instead of the Spirit and let today take priority over your destiny. Cut the drama in your life by learning to listen to and follow the voice of the Spirit.

How to Cut the Drama:

1. *Devote yourself fully to God and quit dancing with the devil.*

2. *Let your future destiny drive your decisions today.*

3. *Make decisions by following the Spirit, not your desires.*

THE TAKEAWAY: Determine to walk in the Spirit today and get rid of the drama in your life.

WEEKEND REFLECTION

"But I say, walk by the Spirit, and you will not gratify the desires of the flesh" (Galatians 5:16).

FOR REFLECTION: If you are led by the Spirit, you won't give in to your own sinful and deceitful desires. The voice you listen to grows stronger. How can you learn to listen to the voice of the Spirit? How can you make the Spirit's voice and influence stronger in your life? Ask God to amplify your ability to hear the voice of the Spirit.

_____

_____

_____

_____

_____

_____

_____

_____

_____

_____

_____

_____

_____

_____

_____

_____

_____

_____

_____

_____

Week Nineteen

MONDAY - Close Enough

THE TEXT: *"Draw near to God, and he will draw near to you"* (James 4:8).

THE TALK: If we want God to draw close to us, we have to draw close to Him. We want God's blessings. We want God's power. But we don't always understand that there's a formula involved. Whoever wants more of God's stuff must first get more of Him. When we delight ourselves in God, He gives us the desires of our heart. And when we delight ourselves in God, what we want most is more of Him. God delights in giving us more of himself, but we have to do our part in drawing close to Him. Seek Him. Pursue Him. Chase after Him. Ask God for more of Himself. When we draw close to Him, He comes running to welcome us home.

Drawing Close to God:

1. *We need more of God if we want more of what He has to give.*

2. *When we delight ourselves in the Lord, we begin to desire more of Him.*

3. *God draws close to us as we draw close to Him.*

THE TAKEAWAY: The closer we get to God, the more we want of Him.

TUESDAY - Clean Hands

THE TEXT: *"Cleanse your hands, you sinners, and purify your hearts, you double-minded"* (James 4:8).

THE TALK: If we want to draw close to God, we have to do it on His terms and not our own. We can't have more of God and more of sin at the same time. Something has to go. If we want more of God, we have to purify ourselves and get our mess out of the way to make space that Jesus can fill. We make our hands clean by repenting from sin and doing what is right and honorable in the eyes of God. We purify our hearts by continuing to walk in the purity Jesus has already given us, retraining our desires so that we want what God wants for us. We do that by pursuing and consuming what is good and honorable to God—things that enhance our purity instead of sullying it. Cleaning our hands and purifying our hearts gets us ready to receive everything God has to offer.

Clean Hands, Pure Heart:

1. *Admit that you are a sinner and confess your sin to God.*

2. *Purify your heart by consuming things that please God— that which is good, honorable, pure, and true.*

3. *Clean your hands by doing what is just and right in God's eyes.*

THE TAKEAWAY: Those with clean hands and a pure heart are ready to receive everything God has to offer.

WEDNESDAY - Wall of Defense

THE TEXT: *"Resist the devil, and he will flee from you"* (James 4:7).

THE TALK: Next to the quarterback, the offensive line has the hardest job in football. The five offensive linemen guard the quarterback, keeping him **safe** and giving him time to make his play. The opposing team has to go through them to get to the quarterback. In the same way, being close to God means the enemy has to go through God to get to us. God gives us space and time to do what we need to do: resist the devil by saying no to sin and yes to God. Like bullies everywhere, Satan prefers soft targets. When we stay within God's protective wall and resist Satan's schemes, the devil doesn't just walk away from us. He runs.

How to Put the Devil on the Run:

1. *Draw close to God so the devil has to go through Him to get through you.*

2. *Let obedience keep you within God's wall of protection.*

3. *Resist the devil by saying no to sin and yes to God.*

THE TAKEAWAY: When you stay within God's wall of protection and resist Satan, you can make the devil turn and run.

THURSDAY - Fall in Formation

THE TEXT: *"You shall march around the city, all the men of war going around the city once. Thus shall you do for six days. Seven priests shall bear seven trumpets of rams' horns before the ark"* (Joshua 6:3-4).

THE TALK: Joshua and his army were ready to conquer Jericho. God gave them the battle plan: march around the city for six days. On the seventh day march around the city seven times, then shout. Before the people went into battle, they had to get into formation.

We have to get into formation if we want to defeat the enemy. Have you ever seen the Army drill team perform? Their level of precision and excellence doesn't happen by accident. Staying in formation takes order, obedience, and dedication. If we want to have victory in our lives, we need to get our lives in formation. All aspects of our lives—friends, finances, and faith—need to be in formation and aligned to God's purposes if we want to see the victory.

Three Ways to Call Your Life into Formation:

1. *Conform your principles according to God's Word.*

2. *Reform your behavior according to God's command.*

3. *Transform your life by aligning with God's purpose and victory.*

THE TAKEAWAY: Get ready for victory by calling your life into formation.

FRIDAY - Really Praise Him

THE TEXT: *"I will bless the Lord at all times; his praise shall continually be in my mouth"* (Psalm 34:1).

THE TALK: We are to bless the Lord at all times. And "all times" means *all times.* God's praise is to continually be on our lips—even in the times we feel like praising Him the least. Our circumstances don't alter God's glory. Even in our darkest moments, God is still good and we should still praise Him because there is power in our praise. Praise can punch through our sadness, worry, and doubt, changing the atmosphere and releasing God's power. Praise can penetrate your persona, giving you a new perspective that allows you to see God's hand at work. And praise promotes God's presence as God indwells the praises of His people. When you don't know what to do, put your praise on and see what God does.

Three Reasons to Praise:

1. *Praise punches through your worry, sadness, and doubt.*

2. *Praise changes your perspective and helps you see God at work.*

3. *Praise promotes God's power and presence in your life.*

THE TAKEAWAY: When life gets hard, put some praise on it.

WEEKEND REFLECTION

"Oh, sing to the Lord a new song; sing to the Lord all the earth!" (Psalm 96:1).

FOR REFLECTION: When God does a new thing in our lives, we should sing a new song. What is God doing in your life? How can you praise Him in a fresh way this week? Who needs to hear your song of praise? Ask God to bless you with creativity so you can sing a new song of praise to Him.

_____

_____

_____

_____

_____

_____

_____

_____

_____

_____

_____

Week Twenty

MONDAY - Chaotic Faith

THE TEXT: *"And we know that for those who love God all things work together for good, for those that are called according to his purpose" (Romans 8:28).*

THE TALK: Have you ever felt like life is spinning out of control? We need faith to see us through the chaos of life. The chaos theory of organizational leadership says that things may seem random and out of control, but that there is order when we look from a higher plane. God is at work for our good in all circumstances, and He is never chaotic or out of control. Think about the movement of the earth. The earth is constantly in motion as it rotates on its axis, tilts with the changing of the seasons, and revolves around the sun. But you never get dizzy because the gravitational pull keeps you in place. In the same way, God is keeping you in place in the middle of your chaos. Cling to your faith. God is working for your good.

Finding Faith in the Middle of Chaos:

1. *Remember that God is in charge.*

2. *Remember that God has a plan.*

3. *Remember that God is working for your good and holding you together.*

THE TAKEAWAY: Cling to faith in the midst of your chaos. God is working for your good.

TUESDAY - Faith Options

THE TEXT: *"He who calls you is faithful; he will surely do it"* *(1 Thessalonians 5:24).*

THE TALK: God keeps His promises. He is faithful, and He wants us to grow in our faith and trust in Him. All other options are inferior to Him. We can look to other people for advice. We can take classes and try to grow our knowledge. We can make plans and devise strategies. And when they all fail, we can think that our problems are insurmountable. But how many times does the Bible say that nothing is impossible for the Lord? Faith teaches us that God is our only option. He is faithful, and we need to learn to look first to Him.

Only One Option:

1. *God is superior to our plans.*

2. *God is superior to our knowledge.*

3. *God is superior to our resources.*

THE TAKEAWAY: When you're running out of options, it's time to have faith. Look first to Him.

WEDNESDAY - Out of Faith

THE TEXT: *"So also faith by itself, if it does not have works, is dead" (James 2:17).*

THE TALK: What do you do when you run out of faith and it feels like the demands of life are more than your faith can carry? Where do you turn when it feels like you've got nowhere left to go? The first thing you need to do is realize faith is your only option. The just shall live by faith. We have no other way to live. When our faith feels weak, we can strengthen it by giving it a purpose. Driving requires faith. When you head out on the highway, you have to believe that the car coming toward you in the other lane is going to obey the laws and not hit your car. Faith requires us to believe the laws and promises of God. Cling to God's promises in the middle of your trial. But we also strengthen our faith by using it. Faith is a verb. Just as courage is doing what's right even when we're afraid, faith is doing what's right even when we doubt. Taking action reins in our doubt and exercises our faith, giving it new life. You are never out of faith. God gives you enough for each moment and each day.

Three Ways to Rekindle Your Faith:

1. *Realize faith is your only choice.*

2. *Repurpose your faith by believing God's promises.*

3. *Rein in your doubt by putting action behind your faith.*

THE TAKEAWAY: Remind yourself that you are not out of faith. God gave you enough for yesterday, and He'll give you enough for today, too.

THURSDAY – Escape Route

THE TEXT: *"No temptation has overtaken you that is not common to man. God is faithful, and he will not let you be tempted beyond your ability, but with the temptation he will also provide the way of escape, that you may be able to endure it" (1 Corinthians 10:13).*

THE TALK: Satan didn't make you do it. He can't. Satan can tempt you, but he has no power to make you do anything. That's good news. You are not alone in your temptations. Temptation is common. There's no temptation you face others haven't faced before. And God is faithful. God won't let you be tempted beyond what you can bear. He always provides a way of escape so you can resist temptation. Look for the escape route God has provided.

Four Ways Out of Temptation:

1. *Memorize Scripture to counter temptation with truth.*

2. *Ask God for help.*

3. *Walk away. Use your feet to get you out of the situation.*

4. *Leverage your accountability. Who holds you accountable?*

THE TAKEAWAY: God always provides a way for you to escape temptation. Look for it.

FRIDAY - Made Up Mind

THE TEXT: *"I am God and there is none like me, declaring the end from the beginning" (Isaiah 46:9-10).*

THE TALK: My mother used to say, "Son, you've got to have a made-up mind if you are going to make it." In other words, once you've decided on something you've got to stick with it. You've got to have a made-up mind. God's mind is made up concerning us. Before you began, God determined what the end of your story would be. God has a plan for you, and your victory is already determined. The enemy may throw things at you, but his attacks will not penetrate your future. God has good thoughts concerning you, and He has decreed your destiny with a made-up mind.

God's Mind Concerning You:

1. *God has already decreed your story will end in victory.*

2. *God has good plans for you that will lead you to your expected end.*

3. *God has placed a shield around you so that the attacks of the enemy will not penetrate your future.*

THE TAKEAWAY: God has made up His mind about you, and His thoughts for you are always good.

WEEKEND REFLECTION

"How precious to me are your thoughts, O God! How vast is the sum of them! If I could count them, they are more than the sand" (Psalm 139:17-18).

FOR REFLECTION: God is always thinking of you. You are never far from God's thoughts. If you could count the number of times God thinks of you, they would outnumber the grains of sand. How does it comfort you to know God is thinking of you? Thank God for His thoughtfulness concerning you, and ask God to reveal His thoughts and plans for your life.

_____

_____

_____

_____

_____

_____

_____

_____

_____

_____

_____

Week Twenty-One

MONDAY - ID Your Haters

THE TEXT: *"Pilate also wrote an inscription and put it on the cross. It read, 'Jesus of Nazareth, the King of the Jews'"* (John 19:19).

THE TALK: The sign Pilate hung on Jesus' cross used the very title the Jewish religious leaders refused to acknowledge: King of the Jews. The Jewish religious leaders were infuriated that Pilate would recognize Jesus this way. They denied and rejected Jesus' identity and rightful authority over them. The religious leaders hated Jesus because recognizing Him as their king would have forced them to relinquish their power.

We have to recognize our haters' motives. Your haters want your jersey. They aren't part of the team. They don't want to play, and they want to take your jersey so you can't play either. The Jewish religious leaders hated Jesus because He could do what they couldn't and reminded them of everything they lacked. Your haters have similar motivations. But the way your haters respond is also your measure of success. Their jeers are really cheers because they mean you are doing well. Every time Jesus did something good, you knew it from the way the haters started booing. Take your haters' boos as affirmation. Your haters can't stop you from achieving your mission. God started you down this path, and your haters can't make you quit.

Recognizing Your Haters:

1. *Your haters are jealous because you can do what they can't.*

2. *Take your haters' jeers as cheers because they mean you're doing well.*

3. *Your haters can only hate. They don't have the power to derail your destiny.*

THE TAKEAWAY: Haters are really confused fans.

TUESDAY - How to Survive Your Haters, Part 1

THE TEXT: *"When the chief priests and the officers saw him, they cried out, 'Crucify him, crucify him!' Pilate said to them, 'Take him yourselves and crucify him, for I find no guilt in him'"* (John 19:6).

THE TALK: The Jewish religious leaders were determined to see Jesus crucified. Jesus had already faced their mockery of a trial. Now they wanted Pilate to do their bidding and put Jesus to death. But Pilate refused—at least initially. Like Jesus, we will also face people who call for our destruction. But we can follow Jesus' example in how we respond. First, don't be caught off guard by the attack. We are soldiers fighting a spiritual battle, and attacks will come. But don't be confused. The real enemy is not your opposition. The real enemy is Satan, and he wants your destruction. So be prepared to fight with spiritual weapons. Don't respond with more hate. Return good for evil and leave the vengeance to God. He will bring justice in His time.

How to Survive Your Haters:

1. *Be prepared. Attacks will come.*

2. *Recognize your real enemy for who he is.*

3. *Keep doing good and trust God to bring justice.*

THE TAKEAWAY: Don't let your enemies make you move. Stand your ground and look for the victory.

WEDNESDAY - How to Survive Your Haters, Part 2

THE TEXT: *"Jesus answered him, 'You would have no authority over me at all unless it had been given you from above'" (John 19:11).*

THE TALK: Jesus stood before Pilate chained, His beard plucked out, a crown of thorns on His head, and beaten beyond all recognition. Pilate could condemn Him to death. But Jesus declared that Pilate had no power over Him. All power belongs to God, and Jesus knew His fate was ultimately in His Father's hands.

Your haters don't have any power over you. They are powerless. God has all power. They can make noise and try to intimidate you, but your fate remains securely in your Father's hands. Your enemy can't hold you any more than Pilate's chains could hold Jesus. Jesus held himself there because it was the part of the Father's plan. Whatever is happening in your life, know God is setting you up so He can set you free. The pain you are feeling now is proof you aren't done yet. You aren't dead. It hasn't killed you yet—and it won't. Your enemies have no power over you. Satan has no power over you. Death has no power over you. Declare it.

How to Survive Your Haters:

1. *Remember that your haters have no power over you.*

2. *Remind yourself that God is setting you up to set you free.*

3. *Declare who's really in control of your life: God, and no one else.*

※

THE TAKEAWAY: Don't let the enemy see you sweat. They don't have any power over you.

THURSDAY - Remember Who Your Enemy Is

THE TEXT: *"For we do not wrestle against flesh and blood but against the rulers, against the authorities, against the cosmic powers over this present darkness, against the spiritual forces of evil in the heavenly places" (Ephesians 6:12).*

THE TALK: Satan is a liar and a manipulator. One of his favorite strategies is to work behind the scenes and try blind us to who our enemy really is. But when trouble comes, we need to remember who we're really fighting: Satan and all his powers of darkness. Our enemies are not our nosy neighbors, the guy at work you can't stand, the child determined to battle you at every turn, or the gossips who enjoy stirring up trouble. Our enemies are not other races, other classes, other philosophies, or other political parties. Satan is the enemy, and Jesus already defeated him at the cross. Don't waste your time fighting the wrong battles. Pick up your spiritual weapons of warfare and take the fight to the real enemy.

Recognizing the Enemy:

1. *Remember that spiritual forces lie behind worldly problems.*

2. *Ask God to open your eyes to the spiritual battle.*

3. *Pick up your weapons and fight, remembering Jesus has already won the victory.*

THE TAKEAWAY: Satan is the real enemy. Take the fight to him.

FRIDAY - Three Steps to Victory

THE TEXT: *"For the Lord your God is he who goes with you to fight for you against your enemies to give you the victory"* (Deuteronomy 20:4).

THE TALK: God used Moses to assure the people of Israel He had guaranteed their victory. Like Israel, we can be active partners in claiming the victory God has already guaranteed. First, make sure what you're going after is worth the fight. Learn to define your win by only fighting battles that matter. Secondly, don't be discouraged by momentary setbacks. Reframe your defeats. What looks like defeat can work toward your victory if you learn from it. Winners don't quit. When you fall, get up and keep fighting until you get your victory.

Three Steps to Victory:

1. *Only fight the battles that matter.*

2. *Reframe your defeat. What can you learn?*

3. *Keep fighting until you win. Victory will come.*

THE TAKEAWAY: You are a winner. Don't quit till you get your victory.

WEEKEND REFLECTION

"To that end keep alert with all perseverance, making supplication for all the saints" (Ephesians 6:18).

FOR REFLECTION: Warriors don't fall asleep on duty. We need to stay alert in our spiritual battle, persevering through prayer. Who needs your prayers today? Don't just say you're going to pray—pray! Ask God to keep you alert and guide you in your prayers.

Week Twenty-Two

MONDAY - Prayer: Answers Guaranteed

THE TEXT: *"If you abide in me, and my words abide in you, ask whatever you wish, and it will be done for you"* (John 15:7).

THE TALK: Abiding is the secret to answer. *Abide* means "to remain" or "to dwell in." If we want to see our prayers answered, we need to remain or dwell in Jesus' presence. It's not a blanket promise. Jesus is not a vending machine. But whatever we ask that flows from His words abiding in us—whatever reflects Jesus' heart and is in accordance with His will—all those things will be done for us. So stay connected to Jesus, and don't be afraid to dream big. God is glorified when you bear much fruit.

How to Get Your Prayers Answered:

1. Stay close to Jesus.

2. Let your prayers flow from your relationship with Him.

3. Pray expectantly, believing it will be done for you.

THE TAKEAWAY: Abiding comes before the answer. Stay close to Jesus and see what God does for you.

TUESDAY - Name Dropping

THE TEXT: *"Whatever you ask in my name, this I will do, that the Father may be glorified in the Son"* (John 14:12).

THE TALK: Knowing the right person can make all the difference in the world. Being able to drop the right name opens doors and gets things done. Jesus' name is the most powerful name in the world. But what does it mean to ask for something in Jesus' name? Asking in Jesus' name means that our requests are consistent with His character. We are asking for Jesus to do that which He already wants and is able to do. When we ask in Jesus' name, things get done because of the reach of His influence and power. And asking in Jesus' name exalts His name, not our own. Things done in Jesus' name bring glory and honor to His name and His name alone. When we pray in Jesus' name, it's not for us. It's for Him.

Asking in Jesus' Name:

1. *Is consistent with Jesus' character.*

2. *Is possible because of His influence and power.*

3. *Brings glory and honor to Him, not to us.*

THE TAKEAWAY: Pray boldly in Jesus' name. What we ask in His name He will do.

WEDNESDAY - Friends, not Servants

THE TEXT: *"No longer do I call you servants, for the servant does not know what His master is doing; but I have called you friends, for all that I have heard from my Father I have made known to you"* (John 15:15).

THE TALK: On the night before He was crucified, Jesus redefined His relationship with His disciples. He wouldn't call them servants any longer. From now on He would call them friends. The difference is that servants follow orders. Friends share one another's hearts. Friends relate as equals, telling one another what they are doing and why. As friends of Christ, Jesus reveals the Father's plans to us. Our understanding of God's plans should underline our prayers, giving us boldness and confidence as our prayers reflect the Father's heart. We don't pray like servants. We pray like friends.

Pray Like Friends:

1. Pray from a position of intimacy and friendship with Jesus.

2. Ask God to reveal the Father's plans to you.

3. Let your prayers reflect the Father's heart and the Father's plans.

THE TAKEAWAY: You are a friend of God. Pray like it.

THURSDAY - Chosen to Bear Fruit

THE TEXT: *"You did not choose me, but I chose you and appointed you that you should go and bear fruit and that your fruit should abide, so that whatever you ask the Father in my name, he may give it to you" (John 15:16).*

THE TALK: We didn't choose God. He chose us. God always takes the initiative in His relationship with us, and He chose us long before we ever thought of choosing Him. God chose us for a purpose: to bear fruit—fruit that would last. God chose you for a God-sized mission. You are tasked with making a difference that will last for eternity. There are truths about God He wants you to declare. People whose lives He wants you to touch. Souls that will be saved because you encountered them and spoke God's Word into their lives. God wants you to accomplish His mission. And because He wants you to be successful, God promises that what we ask in His name He will do. You were chosen for a purpose. Live it out.

Discover Your Purpose:

1. What talents and interests has God given you?

2. How could you use those talents and interests to serve God?

3. *What difference could you make if you served God in this way?*

THE TAKEAWAY: God chose you to bear fruit that will last for eternity.

FRIDAY - Help is on the Way

THE TEXT: *"It is your advantage that I go away, for if I do not go away, the Helper will not come to you. But if I go, I will send him to you"* (John 16:7).

THE TALK: Jesus was leaving. The disciples were scared. They didn't understand what was happening or what Jesus was trying to tell them. But Jesus promised He would not leave them alone. He would send them the Helper—the *paraclete*, "one who walks alongside." The Holy Spirit is our helper and teacher, the Spirit of Christ present with His people. During His earthly ministry, Jesus was limited to only being in one particular place at one particular time. But now through the Holy Spirit, Christ's presence and power is available to all believers at all times, wherever they may be. We need to welcome the Spirit's presence in our lives, living in the Spirit's power, listening to the Spirit, and learning from the Spirit. Through the Holy Spirit the power of Christ dwells within us.

Welcoming the Spirit:

1. *Live by the power of the Spirit.*

2. *Listen to the Spirit's voice.*

3. *Learn what the Spirit has to teach us about the Father.*

THE TAKEAWAY: Welcome the Spirit's power and presence in your life.

WEEKEND REFLECTION

"In the world you will have tribulation. But take heart; I have overcome the world" (John 16:33).

FOR REFLECTION: We shouldn't be surprised when we have problems in this life. Jesus told us that we would. But we can also find courage and hope in the knowledge that Jesus has overcome the world. How does the knowledge that Jesus has overcome give you hope? In what situations in your life do you need to be reminded of God's power and victory? Ask God to give you courage and hope that will help you overcome.

_____

_____

_____

_____

_____

_____

_____

_____

_____

_____

_____

_____

Week Twenty-Three

MONDAY - Your Season

THE TEXT: *"And let us not grow weary of doing good, for in due season we will reap, if we do not give up"* (Galatians 6:9).

THE TALK: One summer I decided it was time to work on our lawn. I got the ground ready, planted the seed, and watered it, but it was a dismal failure. The weeds grew great. The grass didn't. It turns out that summer is the wrong time for planting grass; grass grows in the fall.

Planting and harvesting each have their own seasons. What you plant you will reap. You can't give up. You have to keep watering the plants, fertilizing, and pulling the weeds. You are assured a harvest if you don't quit. The same is true spiritually. What we plant spiritually will produce a harvest at the proper time if we persevere in doing good.

Waiting on Your Season:

1. *Whatever is due is going to come. It's your season. Hang in there.*

2. *Keep planting no matter the season. Plant yourself to get a return.*

3. *Get ready for the harvest by practicing righteousness and doing good.*

THE TAKEAWAY: It's not just a new season—it's your season. Keep planting. The harvest will come.

TUESDAY - Great is the New Good

THE TEXT: *"Whoever believes in me will also do the works that I do, and greater works than these will he do, because I am going to the Father" (John 14:12).*

THE TALK: Jim Collins, leadership expert and author of *From Good to Great*, wrote that the enemy of *great* is *good*. We too easily accept good over great. The same is true spiritually.

Jesus said that those who believe in Him will do even greater works than He did through the power of the Holy Spirit. But we settle for "good enough" too easily. If the power of the Holy Spirit is living inside you, you are already great. Stop accepting mediocrity for yourself. Expect greatness.

Expecting Greatness:

1. *If you want great, don't add anything to God. Good is God with too many O's.*

2. *Good is not good enough. Don't settle. Strive for greatness.*

3. *Attempt great things for God. He told you to expect greatness.*

THE TAKEAWAY: Make "great" a part of your vocabulary. Jesus said you would do great things.

WEDNESDAY - The Journey Begins

THE TEXT: *"Before I formed you in the womb I knew you, and before you were born I consecrated you; I appointed you a prophet to the nations" (Jeremiah 1:5).*

THE TALK: Does your journey seem too long? You thought by now you'd be living your destiny, but you're still in training. You're not alone. Training takes time. God called Jeremiah to prophesy before he was born. His whole life was a training program. Abraham was in training for twenty-five years, Moses for eighty, Daniel for twenty, and Joshua spent forty years as Moses' second fiddle. Sometimes you have to wait on your ministry. Be patient. Your journey has just begun.

Beginning Your Journey:

1. *Let God teach you what you are to speak.*

2. *Deal with your fear. Acknowledge it, but don't let it cripple you.*

3. *Obey God's instructions. He's getting you ready.*

THE TAKEAWAY: God is training you for your ministry. Finish His training program.

THURSDAY - Blessing Blockers

THE TEXT: *"'Return to me and I will return to you,' says the Lord of Hosts"* (Malachi 3:7).

THE TALK: The Jews who had returned from exile didn't understand why life was so hard. Hadn't God promised to bless them? Through the prophet Malachi, God told them the problem was that they had placed blocks in the way of their blessings. Though they claimed to honor God, they were giving Him heart service instead of lip service. They withheld their tithes, offered inferior sacrifices, and did not keep the covenant. God said if they wholeheartedly returned to Him, He would return to them.

We can also put blocks in the way of our blessings. Blessing blockers come in different forms. It may mean raising up an idol in God's place by preferring something else over Him. It may mean giving God lip service by offering only halfhearted obedience. And it may mean hoarding our resources, trusting our money rather than trusting God. If God is not blessing you, it may be that something is in the way. What are the blessing blockers in your life?

Blessing Blockers:

1. *Going through the motions of obedience instead of obeying God with your whole heart.*

2. *Stealing from God by giving your worship, honor, and service to an inferior object.*

3. *Hoarding God's gifts for yourself instead of stewarding them for the kingdom.*

THE TAKEAWAY: God wants to bless you. Get rid of blockers standing in the way of your blessing.

FRIDAY - God's Love Language

THE TEXT: *"For where your treasure is, there your heart will be also" (Matthew 6:21).*

THE TALK: One of the books on marriage I most frequently recommend is *The Five Love Languages* by Gary Chapman. In the book, Chapman describes our love languages as the ways in which we most naturally give and receive love. Some understand love as words of affirmation. Others understand love as quality time. And for some people, gifts, physical touch, or acts of service are the language of the heart. God has love languages, too. God's love languages dictate the flow of our blessings. Learn to speak God's love language and watch your blessings flow.

God's Love Languages:

1. *Quality time: spend time with God in Bible study, worship, and prayer.*

2. *Acts of Service: serve God and God's people.*

3. *Gifts: give time and offerings out of what God has given to you.*

THE TAKEAWAY: Learn to speak God's love languages and watch your blessings flow.

WEEKEND REFLECTION

"Blessed be the God and Father of our Lord Jesus Christ, who has blessed us in Christ with every spiritual blessing in the heavenly places" (Ephesians 1:3).

FOR REFLECTION: God is not stingy in His blessings toward us. He has given us everything, abundantly pouring out every blessing of heaven upon us. How has God blessed you? Make a list of the ways God has blessed you and praise Him for those blessings. Ask God to help you share His blessings with others.

_____

_____

_____

_____

_____

_____

_____

_____

_____

_____

Week Twenty-Four

MONDAY - The Power of Acceptance

THE TEXT: *"And if any place will not receive you and they will not listen to you, when you leave, shake off the dust that is on your feet as a testimony against them"* (Mark 6:11).

THE TALK: As Jesus released His disciples to go spread the news of the kingdom, He gave them instructions for what they were to do when they came to a village. If someone from the town welcomed them, they were to stay with that person. But if a community refused to welcome the disciples and hear their message, they were to leave and shake the dust off their feet as witness of their rejection. That's advice we also need to take as we follow Jesus' commands. Not everyone will accept you and your ministry, so don't get caught up in chasing approval. Once you begin craving the high of acceptance and applause, you become willing to do anything to get it. Don't fall into that trap. When people reject you, shake the dust off your feet and move on. You don't need human approval. You are made in the image of God and are approved by Him.

Approved by God:

1. *God has commissioned you and given you His approval.*

2. *If people reject you and your ministry, they are rejecting the God you serve.*

3. *Seek God's approval and favor, not human applause.*

THE TAKEAWAY: When people reject you, remember God has accepted you as His own.

TUESDAY - Steps to Strengthen Your Journey

THE TEXT: *"Have I not commanded you? Be strong and courageous. Do not be frightened and do not be dismayed, for the Lord your God is with you wherever you go" (Joshua 1:9).*

THE TALK: Joshua had just taken over from Moses as Israel's spiritual leader and military commander. He had the task of finally leading the people across the border to the promised land and claiming their new home. He wanted success, but he was also afraid. God told Joshua not to be afraid. The important factor was not Joshua's strength but God's. Joshua could face the coming battle with courage because God was with Him. And God is with us as we face our battles. The Lord your God is with you. What else do you need?

How to Strengthen Your Journey:

1. *Remember that courage is a command. Fear is only a disguise for lack of faith.*

2. *Risk leads you to reward. If it's not risky, you don't need faith.*

3. *Get out of your feelings and operate on what you know is true: God is with you.*

THE TAKEAWAY: Face your battles with courage. God is with you.

WEDNESDAY - Fear Not

THE TEXT: *"Fear not, for I am with you; be not dismayed, for I am your God" (Isaiah 41:10).*

THE TALK: God is the answer to our fear. He doesn't say, "Fear not, for you are so strong and powerful." Nor does He say, "Fear not, because you are gifted and talented." God tells us not to be afraid because He is with us. When we're afraid, we don't need to look inside ourselves for courage. We need to look to Him. Our God is with us. God's presence gives us all the courage and confidence we need.

Finding Courage:

1. *Don't look for courage in yourself.*

2. *Don't look for courage in your resources.*

3. *Draw close to God and find courage in His presence.*

THE TAKEAWAY: God is with you. Don't be afraid.

THURSDAY - Just for the Record

THE TEXT: *"Moses wrote down their starting places, stage by stage, by command of the Lord" (Numbers 33:2).*

THE TALK: As Israel wandered in the wilderness, God commanded Moses to keep a record of the stages of their journey. We also need to keep a record of what God is doing in our lives. Journaling is important because it helps us record where we've been, what God is showing us now, and the vision God is giving us for our future. We are living records of what God can do, and journaling helps us remember the details so we can tell our story. Journaling also provides a release and a way to talk to God when things aren't going well. Start writing your story.

Three Reasons to Keep a Journal:

1. *Journaling keeps a record of what God is doing in your life.*

2. *Journaling provides a way of release and a way for you to talk to God.*

3. *Journaling prepares you to tell your story.*

THE TAKEAWAY: Jesus bought you with a price, and your story is a bestseller in His eyes. Write your story.

FRIDAY - House Blessings

THE TEXT: *"The Lord has blessed the household of Obed-edom and all that belongs to him, because of the ark of God"* (2 Samuel 6:12).

THE TALK: After David became king over a united Israel, he joyfully set about bringing the ark to Jerusalem. But they did not transport the ark in the way the law required, and one of the men moving the ark died. David was afraid to bring the ark on into Jerusalem, so he left it in a temporary resting place at the home of Obed-edom. The ark was a symbol of the Lord's presence. Obed-edom's home was blessed as long as the ark was there because the Lord was in His home.

We are also blessed when God is in our homes, but we don't have to put a replica of the ark in our living rooms to gain God's blessing. All we have to do is make God welcome in our homes. Invite Him in. Create an atmosphere where God's presence is cultivated and celebrated. Worship God, honor Him, and pray to Him in your home. Make God welcome in your home and you will be blessed.

How to Make God Welcome in Your Home:

1. *Make your home a place of worship.*

2. *Make your home a place of prayer.*

3. *Make your home a place of service.*

THE TAKEAWAY: Welcome the Lord into your home. Ask God to bless your house and everything in it.

WEEKEND REFLECTION

"For there is one God, and one mediator between God and men, the man Christ Jesus" (2 Timothy 2:5).

FOR REFLECTION: Throughout history people have created different ways to get to God. Some rely on acts of service. Others rely on amassing great power or great wealth. And some turn to people they believe are better, holier, or more influential with God somehow. But there is only one God and one mediator between God and humanity: Jesus Christ. Thank God for sending Jesus to make peace between you and God. Ask God how you can help others find Jesus Christ, their mediator and hope.

_____

_____

_____

_____

_____

_____

_____

_____

_____

_____

_____

_____

Week Twenty-Five

MONDAY - Steps to Success

THE TEXT: *"This Book of the Law shall not depart from your mouth, but you shall meditate on it day and night, so that you may be careful to do according to all that is written in it. For then you will make your way prosperous, and then you will have good success"* (Joshua 1:8).

THE TALK: Have you ever wished someone would give you a set of blueprints for success? Joshua did too. As Joshua prepared to lead Israel into battle, God gave Him the prerequisites for success—a set of steps that can also lead to success in our lives. Success begins by meditating on God's Word. In Hebrew, *mediate* means "to chew over." Meditating is more than reading the Bible for five minutes and going about your day. God's Word needs to be chewed on, considered, and carefully digested. But understanding isn't enough. Our actions must reflect our understanding of God's Word. We need to put our understanding into practice, mirroring in our lives what we see in Scripture. As you meditate on and mirror God's Word, watch for the manifestation of God's power in your life. He promises success when we digest and do His Word.

Three Steps to Success:

1. Meditate on God's Word.

2. Mirror God's Word.

3. Watch for the manifestation of God's power in your life.

THE TAKEAWAY: Follow God's commands and walk out success in your life.

TUESDAY - Step into It

THE TEXT: *"Every place that the sole of your foot will tread I have given to you" (Joshua 1:3).*

THE TALK: As Joshua prepared to lead the people into the promised land, God told Joshua that everywhere he walked he would step into His success. What an amazing promise! If you want to step into success, you need to take three different steps. Step forward in faith, believing God will do what He has promised. Step forward in thanksgiving, praising and thanking God for the blessings He has bestowed on you. And step up ready to fight. Satan doesn't give anything away. We have to be ready to fight for our promises. When we walk with the Lord and step forward in faith, God promises us success everywhere we go.

Three Steps of Success:

1. *Step forward in faith.*

2. *Step with thanksgiving*

3. *Step up to the fight.*

THE TAKEAWAY: Step forward with faith and thanksgiving, ready to fight for the success God has promised you.

WEDNESDAY - The Payoff

THE TEXT: *"For the wages of sin is death, but the free gift of God is eternal life in Christ Jesus our Lord" (Romans 6:23).*

THE TALK: If you work, you expect to get paid. Your wages are what you earn for your labor. Death is the payment we earn for the labor of our sin. Sin has a price. It may promise us pleasure, affirmation, or acceptance, but it costs us our souls. Choose who you will work for, because Satan's poison apple payoff will cost you every time. You are worth more than the fool's gold promises he offers. Jesus has bought us for himself with His priceless blood. Satan does not deserve your labor. Why work for the losing side when you can serve the victorious king?

Getting Your Payoff:

1. Don't underestimate the cost of sin.

2. Remember that you are worth more than the wages of your sin.

3. Don't labor for a loser when you could be serving the King.

THE TAKEAWAY: Every day you wake up is a payday. Jesus died to give you eternal life. Live like you just got paid.

THURSDAY – Delay, not Denied

THE TEXT: *"Our soul waits for the Lord; he is our help and our shield" (Psalm 33:20).*

THE TALK: Waiting is hard, but waiting on God's timing is always worth it. Sometimes it takes courage to wait. When you can't see your way out, when you are afraid, or when you don't know where your deliverance is going to come from, it's hard to wait. In the Bible, waiting means to wait expectantly. Pregnancy is a time of waiting, but it's also a time of expectancy. Think about the questions you ask a pregnant woman: "What's the baby's name?" "When are you due?" "Will it be a boy or a girl?" Your questions imply expectancy. The mother isn't just waiting—she's waiting for something. And in the same way, when we're waiting on God, we aren't just waiting. We're waiting for Him to move in His timing. Take courage, and wait for the Lord.

Waiting Well:

1. *Take courage in your waiting.*

2. *Wait with expectancy.*

3. *The delay is meant to prepare you. Get ready for what's coming.*

THE TAKEAWAY: Be determined in your delay. God's coming for you.

FRIDAY – You Betta' Recognize

THE TEXT: *"When the people of Israel saw it, they said to one another, 'What is it?' For they did not know what it was"* *(Exodus 16:15).*

THE TALK: After the Israelites fled Egypt, they were in the wilderness with no way to feed themselves. God provided for His people by sending manna, a kind of bread that covered the ground every morning. It was white like coriander and tasted like wafers made with honey. The people named it "manna," meaning "what is it?", because they had ever seen anything like it before. They had to learn to recognize the miracle for what it was: God's provision for His people. We also need to recognize the miracles in our lives. Open your eyes and see. What manna has God provided for you?

Recognizing Your Miracle:

1. *You are a miracle.*

2. *Your life is a miracle. Stop comparing yourself to others and look at the manna in your life.*

3. *God always supplies you with a miracle for the moment you are in.*

THE TAKEAWAY: Thank God for the miracles and the manna in your life.

WEEKEND REFLECTION

"You keep him in perfect peace whose mind is stayed on you because he trusts in you" (Isaiah 26:3).

FOR REFLECTION: What is your mind fixed on? When we're worried, it's easy to fix our mind on the problems in our life. But we won't find peace that way. Peace comes by fixing our minds on Jesus. What distracts you from Jesus? How could fixing your mind on Him bring you peace? Ask God to help you fix your mind on Him and deepen your trust in Him this week.

_____

_____

_____

_____

_____

_____

_____

_____

_____

_____

Week Twenty-Six

MONDAY - Get the Glory Out of It

THE TEXT: *"So whatever you eat or drink or whatever you do, do all to the glory of God"* (1 Corinthians 10:31).

THE TALK: Our lives should be consumed by God's glory. Our job is to reveal God's power, persona, and essence in our lives and tell of His greatness throughout the earth. Everything we do should point to God's glory. How we handle our problems should reflect God's glory. The expressions of our personality should reflect God's glory. And the purpose of our lives should be to honor and increase God's glory. Who gets the glory in your life?

Getting the Glory:

1. *Let your problems reflect God's glory.*

2. *Let your personality show God's glory.*

3. *Let your purpose increase God's glory.*

THE TAKEAWAY: Take glory on the go and let God get the glory from your life today.

TUESDAY - How to Forgive, Part 1

THE TEXT: *"Then Peter came up and said to him, 'Lord, how often will my brother sin against me and I forgive him? As many as seven times?'"* (Matthew 18:21).

THE TALK: Peter asked the same question many of us ask, even though we know the answer. It's hard to forgive. But it's also essential. Without forgiveness, we stay chained to the people that have wounded us. Forgiveness sets us free. To forgive, start by calculating the debt. Focus on the debt and not your hurt feelings. What do they owe you? What have they taken from you? Once you've calculated the debt, cancel it. Jesus has already canceled your debt on the cross. His payment allows you to cancel the debts of people who have wounded you, too. Say it out loud: "Lord, as you have canceled my debt, so I cancel theirs." Finally, remember that forgiveness is a verb, not a feeling. You may still feel the hurt and the anger. That's okay. The feelings are reminders, not evidence that you didn't forgive. Take the action of forgiving and the feelings will eventually follow.

Steps of Forgiveness:

1. *Calculate the debt.*

2. *Cancel the debt.*

3. *Remember that forgiveness is an action, not a feeling.*

THE TAKEAWAY: Jesus said we are to forgive continually and completely.

WEDNESDAY - How to Forgive, Part 2

THE TEXT: *"Then Peter came up and said to him, 'Lord, how often will my brother sin against me and I forgive him? As many as seven times?'" (Matthew 18:21).*

THE TALK: Forgiveness is an essential tool of faith, but it's an aspect of obedience we often misunderstand. Forgiveness means *for giving*. Forgiveness has been given to us by God and it is now ours to give away. It doesn't matter if they're sorry or if they don't deserve it. God freely and unconditionally forgave our trespasses, and we need to forgive the same way. Forgiveness is for our own good. As it's been said, holding onto unforgiveness is like drinking poison and hoping the other person dies. It destroys us and leaves them unscathed. So, quit holding on to wrongs. Dismiss the case against them and set yourself free. Say it out loud: "Father, I forgive them as you forgive me."

Steps of Forgiveness:

1. *Give forgiveness freely.*

2. *Don't stop the flow of forgiveness.*

3. *Dismiss the case and set yourself free.*

THE TAKEAWAY: Forgive and forge ahead because it's futile to pay back. Pray for their success and blessing.

THURSDAY - In Everything?

THE TEXT: *"Give thanks in all circumstances, for this is the will of God in Christ Jesus for you" (1 Thessalonians 5:18).*

THE TALK: Thanksgiving should be the Christian's state of being. It is God's will for us to be thankful in every circumstance. That preposition is important. God wants us to thank Him in everything, not for everything. We may not be thankful for tragedy or for the consequences of sin in our life, but even in the worst of circumstances we can be thankful that God is there seeing us through. Practicing thanksgiving as a way of life increases God's power in us and allows us to receive more from God. What can you thank God for today?

Practicing Thanksgiving:

1. *Thank God in everything, not for everything.*

2. *Internalizing thanksgiving increases God's power in you.*

3. *Practicing thanksgiving prepares you to receive more from God.*

THE TAKEAWAY: Thanksgiving should be like breathing: a regular, natural, and automatic part of your life. Thank God today.

FRIDAY – The Blessed Life

THE TEXT: *"And all these blessings shall come upon you and overtake you if you follow the voice of the Lord your God"* (Deuteronomy 28:2).

THE TALK: As the children of Israel prepared to enter the promised land, Moses gave them the prescription for how to live a blessed life. Blessing follows obedience. If you want to be blessed, you have to obey. It's that simple. God has given you an assignment. Use everything He puts in your hands to live for Him. Listen to His Word and do what it says. Obedience is the first step toward blessing.

How to Live Blessed:

1. *Obedience ushers in blessing.*

2. *Use everything God puts in your hands to fulfill His assignment for your life.*

3. *Apply God's Word to your life and obey.*

THE TAKEAWAY: Blessing follows obedience. If you want God's blessing, you need to obey.

WEEKEND REFLECTION

"Whatever you do, work heartily, as for the Lord and not for men" (Colossians 3:23).

FOR REFLECTION: Who's your boss? Maybe you're in business for yourself. Maybe you work in a downtown office, a school, or a shop down the street. But whatever your job— whatever you do—you're working for the Lord, not the people around you. It's His approval that matters. What would be different about your life if you remembered that it's the Lord you're working for? How would it change your attitude? Your work ethic? Your enthusiasm? Ask God to let your work be pleasing to Him this week.

_____

_____

_____

_____

_____

_____

_____

_____

_____

_____

_____

_____

_____

DEVOTIONS FOR

Summer

Week Twenty-Seven

MONDAY - He Showed Up

THE TEXT: *"Behold, the virgin shall conceive and bear a son, and they shall call his name Immanuel"* (Matthew 1:23).

THE TALK: Names carry meaning. Jesus' name comes from the Hebrew word *Yeshua*, meaning "God is my salvation." But Jesus also had another name, *Immanuel*, meaning "God is with us." Through Jesus, God drew near to us so He might bring us near to Him. He showed up when we were lost, in the middle of our fear and our pain. Although our sinful mess should have kept Him away, Jesus showed up to stand up on our behalf, redeeming our sin and setting us free. We are not alone. He is still Immanuel: God with us.

God Showed Up:

1. *God came near to us when we could not come near to Him.*

2. *God showed up in person because only He could redeem our mess.*

3. *God showed up to stand up for us, redeem us, and bring us to Him.*

THE TAKEAWAY: God shows up for us. Jesus is Immanuel, God with us.

TUESDAY - Play Your Hand

THE TEXT: *"So I was afraid and I went and hid your talent in the ground. Here you have what is yours"* (Matthew 25:25).

THE TALK: Jesus told a parable about three servants whose master went on a journey. Before he left, the master gave each of his servants a sum of money to steward until his return. The master gave the first servant five talents—an extraordinary amount. A talent was a sum of money worth about twenty years' wages for a laborer. He gave the second two talents, and he gave the third one talent. The first two servants went out and traded with the money, doubling their initial investment. The third servant dug a hole in the ground and hid his master's money. When the master returned, the first two servants showed their master what they had done and received his praise and reward. The third servant told his master that he had hidden the money in the ground because he was afraid. The master was angry with the servant for not investing his funds—not even taking a simple step like putting the money in the bank. Because he had refused to use what he had, the little he had been given was taken away.

In cards and in life we have to play the hand we are dealt. God gives to each of us according to our ability. Some get five talents. Some get one. But unless we are faithful with what has been given to us, we will never receive more. Don't let fear keep you from serving. Play your hand.

Play Your Hand

1. *Don't compare what you've been given. Trust God and steward what you have.*

2. *Prove yourself faithful in small things if you want God to trust you with bigger things.*

3. *Don't let fear keep you from serving. Use what you've been given.*

THE TAKEAWAY: Don't just stand there. Do something. Invest what you've been given and you will get a reward.

WEDNESDAY - Blessed in Your Coming and Going

THE TEXT: *"The Lord will keep your going out and your coming in from this time forth and forevermore" (Psalm 121:8).*

THE TALK: Our family reads this Psalm before we go on a trip. We pray for God to bless us as we go and as we come home. In the Old Testament, *blessing* can mean "to fill," "to make large," or "to anoint with special power." But blessings aren't static. They have to be walked out to be received. Psalm 121 depicts God as a guard who watches over our comings and our goings. He is there when we depart, when we come home, and at every point in between. He ensures the blessing for our journey. But we have to go on the journey to receive it.

Living Blessed:

1. Be blessed when you wake.

2. Be blessed when you work.

3. Be blessed every step of your way.

THE TAKEAWAY: God guards and ensures your blessing. Walk out your blessing.

THURSDAY - Just Say Thank You

THE TEXT: *"For John came neither eating or drinking, and they say 'He has a demon.' The Son of Man came eating and drinking, and they say, 'Look at him! A glutton and a drunkard, a friend of tax collectors and sinners'" (Matthew 12:18-19).*

THE TALK: Our response to Jesus reveals our hearts. The response of the crowds who followed Jesus and John proved they were more interested in a show than the message. The same people who criticized John the Baptist for his ascetic lifestyle criticized Jesus because He ate and drank with sinners. They didn't recognize how the contradiction in their responses revealed their hypocrisy. What does your response to Jesus reveal? Instead of complaining about what He does and when He does it, respond to Him with gratitude and thanksgiving. Jesus died on the cross for you. Thankfulness shows you have received him.

Saying Thanks:

1. *Thank Jesus for what He has done for you.*

2. *Thank Him for what you've been through.*

3. *Thank Him for what you have.*

THE TAKEAWAY: Your response to Jesus reveals your heart. Show gratitude.

FRIDAY - Content but Still Hungry

THE TEXT: *"Not that I am speaking of need, for I have learned in whatever situation I am to be content" (Philippians 4:11).*

THE TALK: Paul learned the secret of contentment in prison. He learned how to be content with what he had. Paul did not lose his contentment because he wasn't free. And he didn't lose his contentment because he was tired, cold, or hungry. His contentment was located in the person of Jesus Christ. Now, Paul still wanted more. He wanted to do more for Jesus. He wanted to preach more boldly. He wanted to see the people he ministered to receive more of God's blessings. He was still striving and pressing on for more, but he was content in his circumstances and thankful for what God had provided. His contentment allowed him to escape the distraction of earthly discomfort and keep looking out for what God was going to do.

How to Practice Contentment While Still Wanting More:

1. *Being content with what you have is not the same as being satisfied with where you are.*

2. *Contentment is a state of mind for your present, not a check on your desires for the future.*

3. *Be careful to be thankful for what you have.*

THE TAKEAWAY: Learn the secret of contentment. Trust Christ for your circumstances and strive toward Him for a better future.

WEEKEND REFLECTION

"Enter his gates with thanksgiving, and his courts with praise! Give thanks to him, bless his name!" (Psalm 100:4).

FOR REFLECTION: Thanksgiving should be part of our worship. We are to come to God grateful and thankful for what He has done. What can you thank God for today? How has He blessed you? How can you show your gratitude to Him? Ask God to show you how to make thankfulness part of your worship.

_____

_____

_____

_____

_____

_____

_____

Week Twenty-Eight

MONDAY - Staring at Your Blessings

THE TEXT: *"And the Lord said to [Moses], 'This is the land of which I swore to Abraham, to Isaac, and to Jacob, 'I will give it to your offspring.' I have let you see it with your eyes, but you shall not go over there'"* (Deuteronomy 34:4).

THE TALK: God let Moses see the blessing of the promised land, but He did not allow him to enter it. Moses had brought Israel to the border, but an act of disobedience kept him from entering the land. We need to be careful lest we only be allowed to stare at our blessings. Sometimes we're too close to our blessing to recognize it. Sometimes we fail to appreciate the gifts of grace we've already been given. And sometimes we stand on the edge of our blessing like Moses, unable to enter its fullness because of harbored sin. Stay close to God, repenting and renewing your relationship with Him. Don't just stare at your blessing—embrace it.

Embracing the Blessing:

1. *Get perspective. Ask God to open your eyes to His blessings.*

2. *Get right. Repent and refuse to harbor unconfessed sin.*

3. *Get close. Draw close to God and cherish your relationship with Him.*

THE TAKEAWAY: Don't get caught just staring at your blessing. Stop staring and start thanking God for what He has done.

TUESDAY - Fighting Faith

THE TEXT: *"Then Elisha prayed and said, 'O Lord, please open his eyes that he may see.' So the Lord opened the eyes of the young man and he saw, and behold, the mountain was full of horses and chariots of fire all around Elisha" (2 Kings 6:17).*

THE TALK: The king of Syria was angry because he could not defeat the army of Israel. As Syria laid ambushes for Israel, God revealed their plans to the prophet Elisha who in turn warned Israel's king. The Syrian king sent his army to surround the town where Elisha was staying, planning to eliminate the troublesome prophet. When Elisha's servant saw the army, he was terrified. But Elisha told the young man not to fear. God had already surrounded Elisha with His heavenly army. The Syrian army was outnumbered.

Your enemies are always outnumbered when God is with you. You still have to fight for your faith, but you never have to fight alone. God's presence ensures your victory.

How to Fight for Your Faith:

1. *Fight for your faith. Satan wants to destroy it.*

2. *Fight with your faith. Your shield of faith defends you against Satan's schemes.*

3. *Fight to get more faith. Battles build your faith and make it stronger.*

THE TAKEAWAY: Don't just fight with your faith—win with your faith. God is with you, and your enemies are outnumbered.

WEDNESDAY - Edible Faith

THE TEXT: *"Be sober-minded; be watchful. Your adversary the devil prowls around like a roaring lion, seeking someone to devour" (1 Peter 5:8).*

THE TALK: Peter warned the church to be on the lookout. Satan was prowling around like a lion, looking for someone to devour. Satan is always hungry, and you look like an appetizing snack to the devil. He wants to destroy you and devour your faith. But don't fret. Satan can prowl and roar, but he can't touch you. He's already defeated. Your faith may feel small, but it's big enough to fight with. That willingness to trust God is all you need. Stand firm. Be courageous and strong. Satan is looking for a snack. Faith means Satan's next snack won't be you.

How Not to be Satan's Snack:

1. Be on alert for Satan's schemes.

2. Remember that your faith is strong enough to defend you.

3. Believe that your faith is dependable enough to deliver you.

4. Resist Satan and watch him flee.

THE TAKEAWAY: Don't be Satan's next snack. Stay alert, stay strong, and let your faith defend you.

THURSDAY - Time to Grow

THE TEXT: *"And Jesus increased in wisdom and stature and in favor with God and man" (Luke 2:52).*

THE TALK: Luke sums up most of what we know of Jesus' childhood in this one verse: Jesus grew. He grew in wisdom, the understanding of God's Word and how to apply it to life. He grew physically. He grew in favor with God and with people. As He grew, God was preparing him for what was to come. Don't despise your seasons of growth. Your growing time is preparing time. Jesus didn't start His public ministry until the right time had come, and God will release you into your ministry when the right time comes for you. In the meantime, use your waiting time to grow. Grow in wisdom. Grow physically, stewarding your health so you can fulfill your calling. Grow in your relationship with God. And grow in your relationships with other people who one day may be part of your team. Your time will come. Don't rush the time you need to grow.

Four Ways to Grow:

1. *Grow in wisdom.*

2. *Grow in health.*

3. *Grow in your relationship with God.*

4. *Grow in your relationships with others.*

THE TAKEAWAY: Don't despise the growing time. Make the most of your season of preparation.

FRIDAY – Prepare for Success

THE TEXT: *"Let your eyes look directly forward, and your gaze be straight before you. Ponder the path of your feet; then all your ways will be sure" (Proverbs 4:25-26).*

THE TALK: You can't prepare for success by looking behind. Let go of your losses and failures. You can't change what's behind you, so you might as well get ready for what's ahead. Keep your eyes fixed on what lies in front of you. Jesus is always ahead, beckoning you closer and leading you into your destiny. Focus on Him. Look at your path and where He's leading you. What steps will lead you closer to Him? What will help you get ready for your destiny? Forget what's behind and strain toward what lies ahead. The finish line is waiting. Look ahead and keep running till you make it home.

Three Ways to Look Ahead:

1. *Let the past go and focus on what's in front of you.*

2. *Look to Jesus and let Him lead you into your destiny.*

3. *Level your path. Do what you need to do to get ready for your destiny.*

THE TAKEAWAY: Forget what lies behind you and focus on what lies ahead. Get ready for your destiny.

WEEKEND REFLECTION

"The wicked flee when no one pursues, but the righteous are bold as a lion" (Proverbs 28:1).

FOR REFLECTION: Righteousness makes you bold. The wicked flee even when no one's chasing them, but the righteous stand strong in the face of opposition. How does righteousness give you courage? How have you witnessed righteous people living boldly and bravely? In what areas do you need to find courage for righteous living? Ask God to give you courage to live righteously for Him.

Week Twenty-Nine

MONDAY - Look Better, Not Back

THE TEXT: *"Forgetting what lies behind and straining forward to what lies ahead, I press on toward the goal for the prize of the upward call of God in Christ Jesus"* (Philippians 3:13-14).

THE TALK: Have you ever noticed that the windshield in your car is bigger than your rearview mirror? You need to know what's behind you, but you can't get where you're going if you keep looking back. Like Paul, we need to forget what lies behind us and strain forward to what lies ahead. God is calling you upward and onward. Stop trying to fix the past and listen to the voice of God. What is He calling you to do? Let God's call define your goal, and don't quit running until you reach the finish line.

Three Ways to Press Ahead:

1. *Leave the past in the past and stop trying to change it.*

2. *Spend more time looking ahead than looking behind.*

3. *Define your goal with God's help. Keep running till you get there.*

THE TAKEAWAY: Don't look back—look better. Keep your eyes on the goal God has for you.

TUESDAY - What were You Thinking?

THE TEXT: *"Keep your heart with all vigilance, for from it flow the springs of life"* (Proverbs 4:23).

THE TALK: Your heart determines the course of your life. In the Bible, the heart is more than just the seat of our emotions. It encompasses our entire inner being—our thoughts, will, emotions, and desires. We must guard our hearts because our hearts direct the course of our lives. One of the most important ways we can guard our hearts is by guarding our thoughts. Don't let negativity take root in your mind. Instead, remix and reboot negative thoughts by meditating on the Word. When your thoughts get stuck in a rut, refresh stale patterns with new revelations of who God is and what He is doing. When your mind races with anxiety or fear, refocus your out-of-control thoughts by taking them captive to God's commands. Set your mind on God and God's will. You are what you think.

Guard Your Thoughts:

1. *Remix negative thoughts with the Word.*

2. *Refresh stale thoughts with new revelations.*

3. *Refocus out-of-control thoughts by taking them captive.*

THE TAKEAWAY: You will not exceed your thought life. Fix your mind on Jesus and His Word.

WEDNESDAY - Fall Forward

THE TEXT: *"Thus says the Lord, 'When men fall, do they not rise again? If one turns away, does he not return?'" (Jeremiah 8:4).*

THE TALK: In the 1996 Olympics, gymnast Keri Strug helped the team clinch the gold medal with a vault that went down in history. Strug fell on her first vault and injured her ankle. The team needed her to stick her second vault to win. She ran, vaulted, and stuck the landing—all on a broken ankle. Falling does not make you a failure. Get back up and get back in the game, using your setback as a setup for your next opportunity. God has made you to win. Don't let failure keep you from your victory.

Three Responses to Failure:

1. *Failing does not make you a failure.*

2. *If you fall, fall forward. Get back up and keep trying.*

3. *Let God turn your setback into a set up for next time.*

THE TAKEAWAY: When you fall, get up, get back in the fight, and get your victory.

THURSDAY - Fighting Words, Part 1

THE TEXT: *"Let the words of my mouth and the meditation of my heart be acceptable in your sight, O Lord, my rock and my redeemer"* (Psalm 19:14).

THE TALK: Our words have power. We need to use them well. Three helpful questions can guide our speech: (1) Will my words start something or stop something? James 3:3-5 says that our words have the power to start a blaze, turn a ship, or control a wild animal. What will your words do? (2) Will my words build something up or tear it down? Your words can build or they can destroy. Use them to encourage others, not tear them down. (3) Will my words create something or copy somebody? Don't just repeat rumors or relay gossip. Creatively speak God's Word into people's lives.

Three Ways to Fight with Your Words:

1. *Let your words start what is good and stop what is bad.*

2. *Use your words to build others up, not tear them down.*

3. *Creatively communicate God's truths instead of repeating gossip and lies.*

THE TAKEAWAY: Your words are weapons. Choose them carefully.

FRIDAY - Fighting Words, Part 2

THE TEXT: *"Let the words of my mouth and the meditation of my heart be acceptable in your sight, O Lord, my rock and my redeemer" (Psalm 19:14).*

THE TALK: Our words reflect what is in us. If we dedicate time to reflect on what is good and honoring to God, our words will reflect those virtues. But if we are dwelling on gossip, impurity, slander, anger, or a host of other sins, we will demonstrate those sins in our speech. If we want our words to be pleasing to God, we must meditate on what is pleasing to Him. Fill your heart with what is good and your words will reflect it.

Acceptable Words:

1. *Watch your words because they reflect your heart.*

2. *Wash your words by filtering what enters your heart.*

3. *Weigh your words by considering the effect they will have.*

THE TAKEAWAY: Words that speak life to yourself and others are always acceptable to God.

Weekend Reflection

"Death and life are in the power of the tongue, and those who love it will eat its fruits" (Proverbs 18:21).

FOR REFLECTION: Your words have the power to speak death or life. Use them well because you will eat the fruit of the words you speak. What have you spoken into being with your words this week? What fruit has come about because of your speech? Ask God to help you speak life.

Week Thirty

MONDAY - Vision for Your Life

THE TEXT: *"Write the vision; make it plain on tablets, so he may run who read it"* (Habakkuk 2:2).

THE TALK: During a tumultuous period in Israel's history, God gave His prophet a vision and told him to write it down. God wanted the vision recorded so those who read it could act on it and prepare for what was going to come. When God gives you a vision for your life, write it down. Writing down the vision allows you to refer back to it and trace the patterns of what God is doing in your life. A written record of the vision helps you develop a strategy and plan to reach it. It makes it real and keeps you from forgetting what God has said He will do. Seek God's vision for your life and write it down. Then use your record to keep yourself on track. Write down the vision God gives you so you can run after Him.

Living the Vision:

1. *Write down God's vision for your life.*

2. *Make a strategy to achieve the vision.*

3. *Use your vision as a roadmap to keep yourself on track.*

THE TAKEAWAY: Write down your vision to keep yourself on track with God's promise. Check your vision today.

TUESDAY - Battling for Your Business

THE TEXT: *"Do not be afraid and do not be dismayed at this great horde, for the battle is not yours but God's"* (2 Chronicles 20:15).

THE TALK: King Jehoshaphat was about to lead the people into a battle. He was outmatched and outnumbered. But God told His people not to be afraid. He would fight on behalf of His people. On the day of battle, Jehoshaphat sent the army out with worship. They didn't lift a finger. God turned the enemy armies against each other. All the people of Judah had to do was pick up the plunder. It took them three days to collect it all. When you think you're outnumbered, remember that God gives the victory. Follow His instructions as you go into battle and wrap yourself in a garment of praise. And get ready to pick up the plunder. When God gives you victory, He'll also give you what's rightfully yours.

Claiming the Victory:

1. *Follow God's instructions for success.*

2. *Take praise with you into battle.*

3. *Prepare to collect the plunder.*

THE TAKEAWAY: Take what belongs to you. Your enemy is already defeated.

WEDNESDAY - Fast Blessings

THE TEXT: *"But when you fast, anoint your head and wash your face, that your fasting may not be seen by others but by your Father who is in secret. And your Father who sees in secret will reward you" (Matthew 6:17-18).*

THE TALK: Jesus didn't say *if* you fast; He said *when* you fast. He assumed that fasting and prayer would both be part of our lives as believers. Sometimes we have to put extra effort in to get our blessing. Fasting is a spiritual discipline. In the Bible, people most frequently fasted from food, but we can also fast from things such as negative thoughts, television, or social media. When we fast, we lay aside distractions to put extra effort into seeking God as we pray expectantly. God answers when we fast and pray.

How to Fast:

1. *Equip yourself for the task. Fasting requires effort.*

2. *Employ your fast by laying aside distractions for a set time.*

3. *Expect God to do something when you fast and pray.*

THE TAKEAWAY: Fasting is a way to put the effort in to get your blessings out.

THURSDAY – My Space

THE TEXT: *"So [Isaac] called its name Rehoboth, saying, 'For now the Lord has made room for us, and we shall be fruitful in the land'"* (Genesis 26:22).

THE TALK: Do your children ever argue about who's touching who or which one took the other's stuff? Some things we don't outgrow. We all want our own space, and sometimes there are people who don't want us to have it. Isaac had a similar problem. The land was so full of Philistines that there was no room for Isaac to grow. Isaac followed his father's footsteps through the land, intending to use the wells Abraham had already dug and which were now rightfully his. But the Philistines were threatened by his presence, and they stopped up and stole Isaac's wells. God told Isaac to dig a new well and helped him make peace with his neighbors. God made room for Isaac in the land, and He still makes room for us.

Finding Your Space:

1. *Keep digging. The water is there. You just have to find it.*

2. *Keep deciding. Follow God's direction.*

3. *Keep declaring. Isaac claimed his territory. Claim what God has given you.*

4. *Keep depending. Trust God to make room for you.*

5. *Keep your destiny. Isaac followed in his father's footsteps. Follow your Father.*

THE TAKEAWAY: Your Father has laid the track down for you. Follow Him to the place He's prepared for you.

FRIDAY - What Goes Around, Comes Around

THE TEXT: *"Give and it will be given to you. Good measure, pressed down, shaken together, running over, will be put into your lap. For with the measure you use it will be measured back to you"* (Luke 6:38).

THE TALK: Relationships have reciprocity. Jesus said that what we give will be given back to us. He was talking about the dynamics of relationships: what we give out comes back to us. When we give generously, we receive generosity. When we give kindness, we receive kindness. But if we give out judgment, hypocrisy, and condemnation, that's what we get back in return. Take care what you dish out. It will come back to you.

It's Coming Back:

1. *If you can't take it, don't dish it out.*

2. *Use your words carefully to build and not destroy.*

3. *If you want a lot, give a lot of your money, yourself, and your time.*

THE TAKEAWAY: What size is your measuring cup? Make sure you can handle what you give out, because it will come back to you.

WEEKEND REFLECTION

"He brought me out into a broad place; he rescued me, because he delighted in me" (Psalm 18:19).

FOR REFLECTION: God is not stingy. He doesn't want you crammed in a corner. He wants you in a broad place where you have room to stretch, move, and grow. Where are some of the "broad places" in your life? Where are some of the tight places in which you want God to give you more room? Ask God to deliver you and lead you into a place broad enough for you to live out your destiny.

_____

_____

_____

_____

_____

_____

_____

_____

_____

_____

_____

_____

_____

_____

Week Thirty-One

MONDAY - The King's Heart

THE TEXT: *"The king's heart is a stream of water in the hand of the Lord; he turns it wherever he will"* (Proverbs 21:1).

THE TALK: Following politics can be disheartening. Leader after leader falls to scandal. Politicians seem more concerned with getting reelected than doing what is best for the nation. Officials at the highest levels of government spew things in press conferences or on their social media feeds that we wouldn't allow our own children to speak. But none of this threatens God's sovereignty. No matter who sits in the Oval Office or controls the chambers of Congress, God is still in control. He can turn the hearts of kings, presidents, judges, and members of congress as He chooses. Take heart: God is in control.

Three Ways to Respond to Government:

1. *Remember that God is in control.*

2. *Pray regularly for those who are in authority.*

3. *Trust God to do what is right in His time.*

THE TAKEAWAY: God is in control. Continue in prayer and trust God to lead.

TUESDAY - Choose Honor

THE TEXT: *"He said to his men, 'The Lord forbid that I should do this thing to my lord, the Lord's anointed, to put out my hand against him, seeing he is the Lord's anointed'"* (1 Samuel 24:6).

THE TALK: David was on the run from Saul when Saul wandered into the very cave where David was hiding. David's men urged him to seize the moment and kill Saul, finally putting an end to his pursuit. But David refused. Although Saul was in many ways an utter failure as king, David still chose to honor him as the Lord's anointed.

We don't always have the privilege of following good leaders. Coaches can be cruel. Bosses can be irrational and capricious. Elected officials can be selfish and incompetent. When we have to serve under a leader who fails to measure up, we can follow David's example. Do what is right, and honor the office even if you can't honor the person holding it.

Acting with Honor:

1. *Pray for those who lead.*

2. *Call for justice and hold leaders accountable, but do it with respect.*

3. *Honor the position when you can't honor the person.*

THE TAKEAWAY: Choose to show honor for the office, even if the person holding it hasn't earned it. God honors our obedience.

WEDNESDAY - Favor in Your Famine

THE TEXT: *"And there was a great famine in Samaria, as they besieged it"* (2 Kings 6:25).

THE TALK: Syria had besieged Samaria, Israel's capitol. No one could come in or out of the city, and the famine was severe. People were so hungry that they ate their own children. The king was angry because the Lord had not intervened, and so he decided to kill the messenger: the prophet Elisha. But as the king's men arrived to take him to the king, Elisha told them that everything was about to change. The Lord would deliver

His people. That night, four lepers decided to hand themselves over to the Syrians and hope for mercy, but when they arrived at the camp, they found it abandoned. God had put fear into the hearts of the Syrian army so that they fled. The lepers returned to Samaria with the news, and the people plundered the Syrian camp. There was enough food to take them from famine to feast. God had delivered His people just as Elisha had said He would.

Don't lose heart in the middle of your famine. Put your hunger to work. Fast from that which holds you back and wait on the Lord's instructions. God will deliver you.

Feasting in Your Famine:

1. *Fast from the stuff that holds you back as you wait for the breakthrough.*

2. *Follow God's instructions even when they don't make sense.*

3. *Forge ahead when God delivers you.*

THE TAKEAWAY: Famines focus you, helping you find more of God and less of what you don't need.

THURSDAY - Prayer: Answers Guaranteed!

THE TEXT: *"Pray without ceasing" (1 Thessalonians 5:17).*

THE TALK: Have you ever prayed and felt like you never got an answer? We need to remember that prayer is about a relationship. Your prayer life reflects the depth of your relationship with God. Prayer is conversation. God wants to hear from us, but we also need to take time to hear from Him. Just as it's rude to hog the conversation and never give your friends a chance to respond, it's impolite to treat God that way too. Listen prayerfully. Cultivate your ability to hear and recognize the Lord's voice. As you grow in your relationship with God, you'll learn to hear the Lord's answer. It may be "Yes." It may be "No." It may be "Wait." But your answer will come.

Three Aspects of Prayer:

1. Prayer is conversational.

2. Prayer is relational.

3. Prayer is personal.

THE TAKEAWAY: Keep praying and listen for your answer. God will answer you.

FRIDAY - Listen to Grow

THE TEXT: *"So faith comes from hearing, and hearing through the word of Christ" (Romans 10:17).*

THE TALK: "Lord, make it stop!" Have you ever shouted that? Sometimes we want the world to stop turning so our problems will go away. But the correct response to our problems is not "Make it stop!" The right answer is "Increase my faith!" We need our faith to grow so we can face the problems in life. What we listen to determines how we grow. Are you listening to the voice of faith or the voice of doubt? Are you tuning your ear to people who live by faith or who live by their own wits? And how often are you listening? Monthly? Weekly? Moment by moment and day by day? If you continually listen to the voice of God, your faith will grow.

Three Ways to Listen:

1. Listen for the voice of faith.

2. Listen to people who walk by faith.

3. Listen to God so you can grow in faith.

THE TAKEAWAY: Turn up the volume on the Word of God to grow your faith.

WEEKEND REFLECTION

"Now faith is the assurance of things hoped for, the conviction of things not seen" (Hebrews 11:1).

For Reflection: Faith is the confidence that what we don't see is as real as what we can. We can't see God. We can't see the move of the Spirit. But we know that God is real and that the Spirit is at work, and our conviction in this truest reality gives us assurance that we do not hope in vain. What strengthens your faith? What helps you keep holding on when hope seems vain? Ask God to grow your faith in Him.

_____

_____

_____

_____

_____

_____

_____

_____

_____

_____

_____

_____

Week Thirty-Two

MONDAY - The Perfect Fit

THE TEXT: *"And the angel said to those who were standing before him, 'Remove the filthy garments from him.' And to him he said, 'Behold, I have taken your iniquity away from you, and I will clothe you with pure vestments'"* (Zechariah 3:4).

THE TALK: The prophet Zechariah saw a vision of God clothing Joshua, the high priest. Joshua was wearing filthy, dirty garments that symbolized his sin. But God removed the dirty clothes and dressed him in clean, fine garments. We never have to exchange God's gifts because He knows us well enough to ensure the perfect fit. God knows the perfect fit for your sin is His grace. The perfect solution for your problems is His power, and the perfect fabric to cover your failures is the salvation of your soul. God removes the rags of your sin and clothes you with His grace. Take a good look in the mirror. Grace looks good on you.

Your Perfect Fit:

1. *The perfect fit for sin is salvation.*

2. *The perfect fit for your troubles is God's power.*

3. *The perfect fit for your failure is God's grace.*

THE TAKEAWAY: God knows your size. His grace is always your perfect fit.

TUESDAY – Just Do It

THE TEXT: *"But someone will say, 'You have faith and I have works.' Show me your faith apart from your works, and I will show you my faith by my works"* (James 2:18).

THE TALK: "Just Do It." You can't go far without seeing the familiar swoosh. The popular Nike slogan is emblazoned on shoes, shirts, and athletic gear of every kind. The brand wants us to believe that greatness comes when we "just do it." Not everyone who picks up a basketball will become the next Michael Jordan, but we know that no one who refuses to try ever will. Greatness requires work. Faith does, too. Faith is action. We can't *feel* faith, we have to *do* faith. Faith requires us to take risks, to step out and trust that God will come through for us like He's promised He will do. We don't show our faith through what we say. We prove it by what we do.

How to Show Faith:

1. *Cooperate with the Holy Spirit.*

2. *Comply with God's Word.*

3. *Expect consequences of your actions—good and bad.*

THE TAKEAWAY: Faith requires action. Live your faith.

WEDNESDAY – Unlimited Possibilities

THE TEXT: *"He said to them, 'Because of your little faith. For truly I say to you, if you have faith like a grain of mustard seed, you will say to this mountain, 'Move from here to there,' and it will move, and nothing will be impossible for you'"* (Matthew 17:20).

THE TALK: It may seem like Jesus contradicted himself in this verse. On one hand Jesus critiqued the disciples for their "little faith," but then He told them that even faith as small as a grain of mustard seed was big enough to move mountains. What was Jesus trying to say? The disciples' problem wasn't that they had little faith—it was that they lacked faith at all. God doesn't require spiritual giants to do great things. Only a mustard seed-sized grain of faith is enough. And seeds are meant to grow. Plant your faith by using it, and watch it grow into a forest of possibility.

How to Plant Your Faith:

1. *Plant the little bit of faith you have.*

2. *Endure the growing season. Seeds are small but durable.*

3. *Use your faith and watch it grow.*

THE TAKEAWAY: When you live by faith, every day is an opportunity for unlimited possibilities with God. Plant your faith and it will grow.

THURSDAY – Facebook Faith

THE TEXT: *"So also faith, if it does not have works, is dead"* (James 2:17).

THE TALK: Social media is almost ubiquitous in today's world. We engage on it because we garner benefit from it—a sense of interaction. But social media doesn't work unless you use it. Faith is the same way. Faith has to be used to live. We have to walk out our faith, using it each day. We have to work out our faith, stretching its influence into every corner of our lives as we work out our salvation. And we have to wait it out when faith doesn't deliver our expected results—trying again until we get it right. Engaging with your faith brings it to life.

Engage with Your Faith:

1. *Walk out your faith.*

2. Work out your faith.

3. Wait out your faith.

THE TAKEAWAY: Your faith has to be used for it to live. Put it to work.

FRIDAY - That Selfie Kind of Faith

THE TEXT: *"For if anyone is a hearer of the word and not a doer, he is like a man who looks intently at his natural face in a mirror. For he looks at himself and goes away and at once forgets what he was like" (James 1:23-24).*

THE TALK: Pay attention at the mall, movie theater, or park, and you'll probably see groups of people taking selfies. They pose just right, hold their phones up, and try to get the perfect angle for an Instagram-worthy pic. Selfies are a way of showing your best self to the world. How foolish would it be to take a selfie, post it to Twitter or Snapchat, and then walk off and forget what you looked like? But we do the same thing with Scripture. Too often we open our Bibles and read, check our devotions off our list, then close the cover without reflecting on what we read. We aren't just meant to hear the word—we're meant to do it. What difference does reading the Bible make in your life?

Doing the Word:

1. Ask what you learned from what you read.

2. Ask what needs to change because of what you read.

3. Ask who else needs to hear a word from what you read.

THE TAKEAWAY: Don't settle for a selfie kind of faith. Do what the Word says.

WEEKEND REFLECTION

"But the one who looks intently into the perfect law, the law of liberty, and perseveres, being no hearer who forgets but a doer who acts, he will be blessed in his doing" (James 1:25).

FOR REFLECTION: We are blessed by doing God's Word. What blessings have you experienced from obeying God's Word? What is one way you can put into practice something you have learned from Scripture this week? Ask God to make you a doer who acts on His word.

_____

_____

_____

_____

_____

_____

_____

_____

_____

_____

_____

_____

_____

_____

Week Thirty-Three

MONDAY - Promised Promises

THE TEXT: *"Let us hold fast the confession of our hope without wavering, for he who promised is faithful" (Hebrews 10:23).*

THE TALK: Promises are only as good as the person who makes the them. You can pinky-swear, make solemn oaths, and sign contracts, but in the end a promise is only guaranteed by the character of the one who made it. We can trust God's promises because He is faithful. Nothing can alter His faithfulness to us or induce Him to break His promise. He won't get a better offer. He won't get tired and give up or get bored and go away. He is faithful, and He keeps His promises to us. For every problem life throws your way, there is a promise from God to meet it. Trust God to complete the process of birthing your promise into reality in His time.

Four Characteristics of God's Promise:

1. *Every promise has a birth.*

2. *Every promise has a process.*

3. *Every promise has a time.*

4. *Every promise has a plan.*

THE TAKEAWAY: There is a promise from God for every problem you face. Trust God to keep His promises.

TUESDAY - Inherit the Promise

THE TEXT: *"So that you may not be sluggish, but imitators of those who through faith and patience inherit the promises"* (Hebrews 6:12).

THE TALK: Faith and patience are the keys to inheriting God's promise. God's promises are woven through the pages of Scripture. Promises for healing. Promises for joy. Promises for your finances, your marriage, and your children. But promises don't happen overnight. We have to persevere, believing in faith God's promise will be fulfilled. Whatever situation you are in, there is a promise of God for you. Search the Scripture to find His promise. Claim it. Believe it. Pray it. Write it down where you can see it and wait expectantly for God's promise to come true. Continue to work as you wait, positioning yourself for the day God's promise is fulfilled. Don't rush it. Trust God's process. He will keep His promise to you.

How to Inherit the Promise:

1. *Name your problem.*

2. *Search the Scripture and claim God's promise.*

3. *Keep working while you wait, getting ready for God's promise to be fulfilled.*

THE TAKEAWAY: Faith and patience are the keys to inheriting God's promise.

WEDNESDAY - Don't Give Up

THE TEXT: *"And there was a widow in that city who kept coming to him and saying, 'Give me justice against my adversary'"* (Luke 18:3).

THE TALK: Jesus told a parable about a widow and an unjust judge. The judge initially refused to give her what she wanted, but her persistence wore him down. He gave the woman justice so she would not wear him out with her constant coming. If persistence can sway an unjust judge, how much more will persistence impact our loving Father? God desires justice for His people. He wants to bless us. Your problems cannot outlast God's promise. Don't give up. Persevere in prayer and keep asking God for what is yours. He will answer you.

Keep Asking

1. *Ask expectantly.*

2. *Ask with thanksgiving.*

3. *Ask with heartfelt belief.*

THE TAKEAWAY: Don't give up. God will keep His promise to you.

THURSDAY - Keep Running

THE TEXT: *"Let us also lay aside every weight, and sin which clings so closely, and let us run with endurance the race that is set before us"* (Hebrews 12:1).

THE TALK: Doing the right thing can get tiring. You tithe, but you don't see the blessing. You go to work, but the promotion doesn't come. You tell your children to behave, but they keep getting in trouble for the same things they did the day before. Sometimes the weight you carry grows so heavy that it seems easier to stop and sit down right where you are, but you can't win the race by quitting. Get rid of the sin that holds you back. Toss off the burdens that weigh you down. Maybe your legs are tired. Maybe your arms feel week. But keep running—keep doing the next right thing and the next one after that. Jesus is waiting for you at the finish line, and He promises you the victory.

How to Keep Running:

1. Get rid of the sin that holds you back.

2. Keep your feet moving and do the next right thing.

3. Look to the finish line. Jesus is waiting.

THE TAKEAWAY: Jesus has promised you the victory. Keep running until you get to Him.

FRIDAY - Visible Perseverance

THE TEXT: *"I know your works, your toil and your patient endurance" (Revelation 2:2).*

THE TALK: Never fear that God doesn't see what you're going through. He does. He knows how hard you work. He knows the struggles that you face. And He knows that you are enduring patiently as you wait for His promise to be fulfilled. He sees you. Don't lose hope, thinking you are abandoned. Don't give in to compromise or secret sin. Persevere. Keep fighting. Keep believing. Keep proclaiming the truth. God sees you, and He will keep His promise to you.

God Sees You:

1. God sees your struggles.

2. God sees your fears.

3. God sees your work, your labor, and your perseverance.

THE TAKEAWAY: Don't give up. God sees you, and He will keep His promise to you.

WEEKEND REFLECTION

"The Lord is not slow to fulfill His promise as some count slowness, but is patient toward you, not wishing that any should perish but that all should reach repentance" (2 Peter 3:9).

FOR REFLECTION: God is not slow in keeping His promises. He will return, but He is waiting until all have a chance to repent. His timing is perfect—both the timing of His return, and His timing for keeping promises in your life. What promises of God are you waiting on? How does it encourage you to know that God is not slow about keeping His promise? Ask God to help you persevere as you wait on His promise to be fulfilled.

_____

_____

_____

_____

_____

_____

_____

_____

_____

_____

_____

_____

_____

Week Thirty-Four

MONDAY - If Only I Had

THE TEXT: *"Peter again denied it, and at once a rooster crowed"* (John 18:27).

THE TALK: Jesus had said Peter would deny Him. Peter refused to believe it until it happened. In the end, all it took was a few questions for Peter to deny following Jesus. When he realized what he had done, he was overcome with sorrow. Do you know the sting of regret? We all have things we wish we had—or hadn't—done. But regret can lead to restoration. Jesus forgave and restored Peter, and He will forgive and restore you.

The Power of Regret:

1. *Let regret remind you of Jesus' forgiving power.*

2. *Let regret fuel your future and work for your good.*

3. *Let regret lead to your restoration.*

THE TAKEAWAY: Don't wallow in regret. Let your regret lead you to restoration.

TUESDAY - Bounce Back from Your Setback

THE TEXT: *"Jesus said to them, 'Children, do you have any fish?'"* (John 21:5).

THE TALK: After Jesus died and was buried, the disciples didn't know what to do. Even after the resurrection they still couldn't make sense of it all. And so they returned to what was familiar: their old occupation of fishing. But Jesus found them there. They didn't recognize Him at first, but Jesus told them where to catch fish. And the miracle that followed showed them it was the Lord. They had failed, but Jesus didn't give up on them. He was using their setback as a setup for a new beginning. Don't let your failures end your mission. Bounce back. God's not done with you.

When You Fail:

1. *Keep your eyes open for Jesus. He's coming for you.*

2. *Keep working. Failing doesn't end your mission.*

3. *Keep trying. Jesus will use your setback to set you up for a new beginning.*

THE TAKEAWAY: Failure doesn't mean you're through. Look for the new beginning Jesus is bringing to you.

WEDNESDAY - How Deep is Your Love?

THE TEXT: *"Peter was grieved because he said to him the third time, 'Do you love me?'" (John 21:17).*

THE TALK: Peter denied Jesus three times on the night He was crucified. After the resurrection, Jesus restored Peter. Jesus asked Peter "Do you love me?" three times. Peter was deeply grieved, but Jesus needed to measure the depth of Peter's love so He knew Peter could handle the task ahead. Peter would lead the fledgling church, shepherding the flock Jesus had entrusted to him, and Peter's mission would eventually lead him to his own cross. Jesus flipped the script. Sometimes He flips the script on us, too. We know Jesus died for us, but are we willing to die for Him? Is your love deep enough for you to handle the mission God has for you?

Deepen Your Love:

1. *Be willing to go past lip service to a deeper level of love.*

2. *Strive to live a life worthy of Christ's love.*

3. *Develop a love that lasts through thick and thin.*

THE TAKEAWAY: Develop a love for Jesus deep enough to sustain you on the mission He has for you.

THURSDAY - Does God Play Favorites?

THE TEXT: *"Peter turned and saw the disciple whom Jesus loved following them, the one who also had leaned back against him during the supper . . . When Peter saw him, he said to Jesus, 'Lord, what about this man?'" (John 21:20-21).*

THE TALK: God's plans are not one-size-fits-all. God's plan for you is not the same as God's plan for me. Different plans don't mean one person's plan is better than another's; God's plans for each of us are different because God has made each of us unique. We all have our own stories, talents, gifts, and abilities, and God intends to use each of us for His glory just as He has designed us to be. God's plans are tailored to fit. His plan for you won't fit anyone else, and you can't squeeze yourself into the shape of anyone else's plan. Don't fall into the comparison trap or fret that God's plans for someone else are better than His plans for you. God doesn't give out anything but the best. Trust Him.

Working the Plan:

1. *Believe that God has a personal plan for you.*

2. *Trust God to reveal His plan for you in His time.*

3. *Work your plan—not anyone else's.*

THE TAKEAWAY: God doesn't play favorites. We all get His best.

FRIDAY - Your Blessing Has Your Name on It

THE TEXT: *"Jesus said to him, 'If it is my will that he remain until I come, what is that to you? You follow me!'" (John 21:22).*

THE TALK: After the resurrection, Jesus called Peter to his life's work. Peter received his call, but then he wanted to know what plans Jesus had for John. Jesus told him John's calling wasn't any concern of his. Peter's job was to follow Jesus.

Your blessing has your name on it and nobody else's. Your neighbor's calling has no impact on your blessing. Their success or failure will not affect the size of your blessing. Don't worry about what God is calling them to do. Listen to what He is calling you to do and obey. Your job is to follow Jesus. That's the only way you will ever see your blessing.

Receive Your Blessing:

1. *Pay attention to what Jesus will do for you.*

2. *Put an end to your worries about what Jesus is doing for others.*

3. *Place your eyes on following Jesus.*

THE TAKEAWAY: Nobody else can get what God has for you. Don't worry about them. Follow Jesus.

WEEKEND REFLECTION

"That you, being rooted and grounded in love, may have strength to comprehend with all the saints what is the breadth and length and height and depth, and to know the love of Christ that surpasses knowledge, that you may be filled with all the fullness of Christ" (Ephesians 3:17-20).

FOR REFLECTION: If we want to be filled with Christ's power, we need to know the fullness of His love. How has Christ demonstrated His love for you? How is His love evident in your life? Ask God to help you comprehend the full measure of Christ's love so you may be filled with the fullness of Christ's power.

Week Thirty-Five

MONDAY - The Struggle is Real

THE TEXT: *"But as servants of God we commend ourselves in every way: by great endurance, in afflictions, hardships, calamities, beatings, imprisonments, riots, labors, sleepless nights, [and] hunger" (2 Corinthians 6:4-5).*

THE TALK: Following God doesn't exempt us from hard times, but it does mean God gives us the power to get through them. Don't be surprised when hard times come. Difficulties are part of living. Instead, determine to follow Paul's example in demonstrating faith, hope, and love even as you endure. Remember, we live in a parallel world. Our true citizenship is in the kingdom of God. The sorrows of this world are nothing compared to heaven's reward.

Three Ways to Respond to Hard Times:

1. *Determine to endure.*

2. *Live like a citizen of God's kingdom.*

3. *Look forward to heaven's reward.*

THE TAKEAWAY: We can endure the difficulties of this life knowing we have a greater reward waiting for us in Christ's kingdom.

TUESDAY - Hope for the Crippled Soul

THE TEXT: *"So Mephibosheth lived in Jerusalem, for he ate always at the king's table. Now he was lame in both feet" (2 Samuel 9:13).*

THE TALK: It was a long, hard road before David became king. Saul, Israel's first king, was so jealous of David's power and popularity that he tried to kill him. David fled from Saul, but he made a covenant of friendship with Saul's son, Jonathan. After Saul and Jonathan died in battle with the Philistines, David became king over all Israel. Once he had secured the throne, David looked for a member of Saul's family whom he could show kindness for Jonathan's sake. Jonathan had one surviving son, Mephibosheth, who was lame in both feet. David made him heir to all of Saul's property and brought Mephibosheth to Jerusalem to eat at the king's table.

As the crippled grandson of the former king, Mephibosheth had no power or standing. But David's covenant with his father changed everything. Maybe you feel crippled, abandoned, worthless, and forgotten, but God has made a covenant with you through Jesus, and that covenant changes everything. You have a seat at the King's table. Get yourself to the table, and live like a child of the King.

Three Sources of Hope for a Crippled Soul:

1. *God has not forgotten you.*

2. *Covenant changes everything.*

3. *You have a seat at the King's table.*

THE TAKEAWAY: God has not forgotten you. He has redeemed you. You are a child of the King.

WEDNESDAY - Coping Skills

THE TEXT: *"We are afflicted in every way, but not crushed; perplexed, but not driven to despair; persecuted, but not forsaken; struck down, but not destroyed" (2 Corinthians 4:8).*

THE TALK: Paul was no stranger to suffering. But instead of destroying him, Paul's sufferings made him stronger. Paul developed plug-and-play coping skills. When trouble came, he didn't have to run around to get advice or wonder what to do. His walk with God and knowledge of the Word had sunk so deeply into his life that he could automatically respond to difficulty out of the depth of his relationship with God. He kept an eternal perspective, looking forward to the glory to come. And Paul relied on the power of faith, knowing God would not let him down. Paul's coping skills allowed him to avoid snapping under pressure and finish strong.

Three Responses to Suffering:

1. *Develop plug-and-play coping skills.*

2. *Put difficulties in perspective.*

3. *Draw on God's power.*

THE TAKEAWAY: Dig deep into your relationship with God to cultivate the coping skills of perseverance, perspective, and power.

THURSDAY - Don't Waste Your Pain

THE TEXT: *"Blessed be the God and Father of our Lord Jesus Christ, the Father of mercies and God of all comfort, who comforts us in all our affliction, so that we may be able to comfort those who are in any affliction, with the comfort with which we ourselves are comforted by God" (2 Corinthians 1:3-4).*

THE TALK: The pain in our life is never without purpose. When God comforts us in our pain, we can share that comfort with others. If you're going through a hard season now, know your pain is not permanent. Look for who God wants to be with you in this season. How is God bringing you comfort? Once you've experienced God's comfort, look for the purpose. Don't waste your pain. Let God use the pain of your past to bring comfort to others in the present. Pass on your healing.

Three Ways to Find Purpose in Pain:

1. *Remember pain is not permanent.*

2. *Don't waste your pain. Look for the purpose.*

3. *Pass on your healing.*

THE TAKEAWAY: Give your pain an assignment. People around you are hurting. Look for ways to pass on your healing and share God's comfort with them.

FRIDAY - Straight Outta Patience

THE TEXT: *"And let steadfastness have its full effect, that you may be perfect and complete, lacking in nothing" (James 1:4).*

THE TALK: Waiting is hard. But steadfastness—patience—has a job to do in your life. Every great leader has a season of preparation and waiting. As patience does its work in us, our passion and purpose grow, preparing us for the day of release God has chosen. Patience is a jackhammer which penetrates the places in our lives that need work. God uses patience in our seasons of obscurity, dealing with our immaturity and getting us ready for what He has in store. Don't rush God's work. He knows what time it is, and He's getting you ready for your moment to shine.

Three Powers of Patience:

1. *Patience grows you.*

2. *Patience penetrates you.*

3. *Patience prepares you.*

THE TAKEAWAY: Set your clock on patience. Persevere with persistence, trusting that God knows what time it really is in your life.

WEEKEND REFLECTION - Treasured Tears

"You have kept count of my tossings; put my tears in your bottle. Are they not in your book?" (Psalm 56:8).

FOR REFLECTION: Your tears are not wasted. God stores them in His bottle and records them in His book. He sees your pain, and He will redeem it. How have you seen God bring purpose out of your pain? How does knowing God remembers and promises to redeem your suffering help you endure?

_____

_____

_____

_____

_____

_____

_____

_____

_____

_____

_____

_____

Week Thirty-Six

MONDAY - What Next?

THE TEXT: *"And Gideon said to him, 'Please sir, if the Lord is with us, why then has all this happened to us?'"* (Judges 6:13).

THE TALK: Israel was under siege from the Midianites. The Midianites stole the Israelite crops and livestock and laid waste to the land. And like the rest of his people, Gideon wondered why God was letting it all happen. Have you ever asked that question? When we are in pain and it feels like life is falling apart, it's a natural response. But just because mess is happening in your life doesn't mean God has forgotten you. He's still there. Take whatever strength you have to stand. Get over your weaknesses—God is going with you, and in your weakness He is strong. He will give you a sign and show you what to do. You may never know why. But God is with you and He will deliver you.

Steps to Take:

1. *Go in your strength.*

2. *Get over your weaknesses.*

3. *Remember God is going with you.*

4. *Look for the sign God will give you.*

THE TAKEAWAY: Whatever happens next, God's got you.

TUESDAY - Bent Over

THE TEXT: *"And behold, there was a woman who had had a disabling spirit for eighteen years. She was bent over and could not fully straighten herself" (Luke 13:11).*

THE TALK: As Jesus taught in the synagogue, there was a woman present who had been crippled by an evil spirit for eighteen years. Jesus set her free and healed her so she was able to stand upright. The synagogue ruler complained because He was healing on the Sabbath, but Jesus rebuked him. The Sabbath was a day of rest and freedom—the perfect day for the Savior to set people free.

Maybe you know what it's like to feel bent over and weighed down. Finances, relationships, spiritual sickness—whatever the symptom, the load has you bent over and weighed down. Jesus offers you freedom. People may grumble. Let them. Move forward in your condition and come to Jesus. And when Jesus tells you to stand, raise your chin and straighten your back. Jesus has delivered you. Stand like you've been set free.

Stand Tall:

1. *Endure the public talk as you make your way to the Savior.*

2. *Endeavour to move forward in your condition.*

3. *Embrace your freedom and stand tall when Jesus gives you the command.*

THE TAKEAWAY: Standing up is spiritual, not just physical.

WEDNESDAY - God's Got You

THE TEXT: *"He has said, 'I will never leave you nor forsake you'" (Hebrews 13:5).*

THE TALK: God has plans to deliver you to your destiny, but God is also interested in the process that gets you there. He may not move in what we think is a straight line, but He has promised that He will never leave us alone. Trusting God's process can be tough for those of us who are bottom-line, end-results type of people. When we value the destination more than the journey, it can feel like we're butting heads with God. But God is interested in more than the endpoint of your journey. He wants to build your character along the way so you're ready for release when it comes. And He will never leave you alone. God knows the end from the beginning. Trust Him to get you there.

Enjoying the Journey:

1. *Remember that it's not just about where you're going but how you get there.*

2. *Ask God how He wants to transform your character through the journey.*

3. *Believe that He will be with you every step of the way.*

THE TAKEAWAY: Process matters. Let God build you along the journey. He won't leave you alone.

THURSDAY - What Now?

THE TEXT: *"If any of you lacks wisdom, let him ask God, who gives generously to all without reproach, and it will be given him"* (James 1:5).

THE TALK: Have you ever been caught in a situation where you didn't know what to do? Maybe it felt like there were no good options. Or maybe it seemed like all the options were good, and you needed to know what was best. The good news is that God has all the answers. If we need wisdom, we only need to ask Him. He gives generously to all without reproach. When you're wondering, "What now?", all you have to do is ask.

How to Ask for Wisdom:

1. *Admit you need instruction.*

2. *Ask for directions.*

3. *Accept your new directions*

THE TAKEAWAY: When you need wisdom, ask God. He won't judge you for not knowing the answer.

FRIDAY - The Order of the Day

THE TEXT: *"But seek first the kingdom of God and his righteousness, and all these things will be added to you"* (Matthew 6:33).

THE TALK: Life has a certain order to it. You have to crawl before you can walk. You have to go to kindergarten before you can go to college. And you've got to get a few falls out of the way before you ever learn to ride a bike. There's an order to spiritual things as well, though it may seem counterintuitive to us: Kingdom First. Our first priority is to be the kingdom of God. But our temptation is to push the kingdom aside as we tend to things that feel more urgent—what we're going to eat and drink, what our plans are for tomorrow, or the ever-present list of worries that occupy our minds and hearts. But God promises that when we seek His kingdom first, He'll take care of the rest for us. If you want to get your life together, learn to follow God's kingdom order. When we follow God's order of operations, we find peace.

Finding Order:

1. *God's order supersedes the natural order.*

2. *"Don't worry" is a spiritual command we must obey.*

3. *Following God's kingdom order aligns our lives with God's purpose and releases His power to provide.*

THE TAKEAWAY: Get your life in God's kingdom order and you will have everything you need.

WEEKEND REFLECTION

"Strength and dignity are her clothing, and she laughs at the time to come" (Proverbs 31:25).

FOR REFLECTION: The wise woman described in Proverbs 31 laughs without fear of the future. Because she fears the Lord, she doesn't have to fear the future. We can face the future without fear when we know God holds the future in His hands. What aspects of your future tempt you to fear? How can you remind yourself that God has those things under control? Ask God to help you learn to fear Him so you can laugh at the days to come.

_____

_____

_____

_____

_____

_____

_____

_____

_____

_____

Week Thirty-Seven

MONDAY - Citizens of Heaven

THE TEXT: *"But our citizenship is in heaven, and from it we await a Savior, the Lord Jesus Christ" (Philippians 3:20).*

THE TALK: I spent twenty-one and a half years in military service. I love and honor my country, but I am a citizen of heaven. It is good to honor and respect our country and its symbols, but we can't equate patriotism with Christianity. Jesus didn't come only for America—He came for the world. When we gather in heaven, we aren't going to honor the red, white, and blue. We will worship the lamb who was slain—and we will worship together with people from every nation. As we think about what patriotism means, we need to be careful not to let the flag take the place of the cross. Maybe you want to stand when the anthem is played. Maybe you feel it's best to kneel. Honor the flag and call for justice in the way that is most appropriate for you, but respect other people's freedoms to express themselves differently. Don't worship the flag. Worship Jesus.

Citizens of Heaven:

1. *Are loyal to a greater king.*

2. *Keep their focus on building the kingdom of heaven, not this world.*

3. *Worship Jesus and Jesus alone.*

THE TAKEAWAY: Don't let the flag cover up the cross. You are a citizen of heaven. Worship Jesus.

TUESDAY - What is Caesar's?

THE TEXT: *"He said to them, 'Then render to Caesar the things that are Caesar's, and to God the things that are God's'" (Luke 20:25).*

THE TALK: The Jewish leaders thought they had Jesus in a tight spot. If Jesus said they shouldn't pay taxes to Caesar, it would make Him an enemy of Rome. But if He said they should, Jews longing for independence would reject His teaching. Jesus asked them to show Him a coin and identify whose image was on it. The coin was stamped with Caesar's image. Jesus told them to give to Caesar what was Caesar's and give to God what was God's.

It seems some Christians today are confused about what belongs to Caesar and what belongs to God. We need to sort out what it means to be followers of Christ in a nation that does not follow Him. It's not a new position. The church was birthed under the authority and corruption of Rome, and only a handful of the forty-two biblical kings feared the Lord. We need to give our nation what it is due: respect for our leaders, obedience to laws, and the taxes we rightfully owe. But we must also give God what He is due: the full allegiance and obedience of our hearts. Obeying God requires us to call for justice, to hold our leaders accountable, and to keep lifting our voices to advocate for change. Give Caesar what is His, but give God everything.

Four Actions to Take:

1. *Pray.*

2. *Participate in peaceful protest.*

3. *Contribute to positive dialogue.*

4. *Put your politicians on notice and hold them accountable.*

THE TAKEAWAY: Give Caesar what he is due, but give God your heart.

WEDNESDAY - Prosperous Position

THE TEXT: *"She said, 'Yes, Lord, yet even the dogs eat the crumbs that fall from their masters' table'"* (Matthew 15:27).

THE TALK: One day as Jesus was ministering in a predominantly Gentile area, a Canaanite woman began begging Him to heal her daughter. The disciples asked Jesus to send her away, but the woman kept asking for His help. At first Jesus said that He was sent only to the people of Israel. During His earthly ministry, Jesus' focus was on ministering to the Jews, who would then take the gospel to the world. But God's heart has always been for all people. Jesus recognized the woman's tenacious faith and wanted to reveal it to the disciples. His comments encouraged her to persist, and the woman fell at Jesus' feet and repeated her request. Jesus praised the woman for her faith and her daughter was healed. Don't let rejection stop you from coming to Jesus. Let persistence demonstrate your faith, and position yourself so you are ready to receive Jesus' provision for you.

Get Ready to Receive:

1. Don't let rejection keep you away.

2. Persist in prayer and keep repeating your request with expectation.

3. Position yourself in submission to Jesus so you are ready to receive from Him.

THE TAKEAWAY: Let your persistence show your faith, and position yourself so you are ready to receive.

THURSDAY - The Purpose of Passion

THE TEXT: *"You shall love the Lord your God with all your heart and with all your soul and with all your might"* (Deuteronomy 6:5).

THE TALK: We are created for passion. We are passionate about our favorite sports teams, hobbies, and causes. We are passionate about the people we love. But God gave us passion for a purpose. Our passion should be centered on Him. Our passion for God leads us into the future He has promised for us. It keeps us focused and delivers us from the temptation to do wrong. Passion for God should be the defining characteristic of our lives, the plumb line that brings everything else into alignment. Check your passion. Are you using it for God's purpose?

The Purpose of Passion:

1. Passion for God prepares you for your promised future.

2. Passion for God delivers you under pressure.

3. Passion for God keeps you focused and prevents you from getting off track.

THE TAKEAWAY: Passion for God will penetrate your problems and bring purpose to your life.

FRIDAY - As You Walk

THE TEXT: "You shall teach them diligently to your children, and shall talk of them when you sit in your house, and when you walk by the way, and when you lie down, and when you rise" (Deuteronomy 6:7).

THE TALK: As Moses reminded Israel of God's commands, He stressed the importance of teaching the next generation. God wants us to disciple our children. Bringing them to church is important, but spiritually nurturing our children isn't only a Sunday morning job. If we want our children to grow strong in the Lord, they need to see us embrace God's Word in every aspect of our lives. Teach them diligently. Talk about God's commands at home. Discuss Scripture as you go about your days. Let the words of God be the last thing on your lips as you kiss your children goodnight and the first words you say as you wake them up in the morning. Your children's faith will grow as they see faith in you.

Teach Them Diligently:

1. *Make time to teach your children about God.*

2. *Incorporate Scripture into every part of life.*

3. *Build discipling your children into your daily routine.*

THE TAKEAWAY: We are responsible for nurturing our children's faith. Teach them well.

WEEKEND REFLECTION

"When words are many, transgression is not lacking, but whoever restrains his lips is prudent" (Proverbs 10:19).

FOR REFLECTION: Most of us talk more than we should. Sometimes it's because silence is scary. Sometimes it's because social media invites us to shout our opinions to the corners of the earth. Too many words can lead us to sin. Wisdom appreciates the power of silence. When have you spoken this week when you should have remained silent? How can restraining your lips keep you from sinning? Ask God to show you when to speak and when to remain silent so your words don't lead you into sin.

Week Thirty-Eight

MONDAY - Birthing Out of Barrenness

THE TEXT: *"Is anything too hard for the Lord? At the appointed time I will return to you, about this time next year, and Sarah shall have a son"* (Genesis 18:14).

THE TALK: One day God came and met with Abraham. God told Abraham that he and his wife Sarah would have a son. Sarah was listening from a tent nearby and laughed when she heard. She was an old, barren woman and her husband was old. Having a child at her age was an impossibility. But nothing is too hard for the Lord, and God kept His promise. When Abraham was 100 and Sarah was 90, they had a son. They named him Isaac, meaning "laughter." Nothing is too hard for the Lord—even bringing a birth out of your barrenness. The pains and pressures of life may mean your delivery day is near. Trust Him to deliver you.

Birth from Barrenness:

1. *Your delivery date comes when God shows up.*

2. *Your pain, problems, and pressures are birth pains—signs your delivery is near.*

3. *Don't laugh. God can turn your doubt into a delivery.*

THE TAKEAWAY: Nothing is impossible for God. Let Him turn your barrenness into a birth.

TUESDAY – Don't Worry, Be Happy

THE TEXT: *"Therefore, do not be anxious about tomorrow, for tomorrow will be anxious for itself. Sufficient for the day is its own trouble" (Matthew 6:34).*

THE TALK: Worry wears you down and takes a physical toll. High blood pressure, diabetes, heart problems, and insomnia can all result from anxiety. You were not made to worry. You were made to trust and communicate with God. Worry accomplishes nothing, but prayer accomplishes everything. Don't worry. Pray and trust God.

When You Worry:

1. *Place your hopes in God's hands.*

2. *Place your fears in God's hands.*

3. *Place your thoughts in God's hands.*

THE TAKEAWAY: Worry does nothing, but prayer does everything. Don't worry—pray. If you prayed about it, don't worry about it.

WEDNESDAY – Naked Worship

THE TEXT: *"He said, 'Who told you that you were naked? Have you eaten of the tree of which I commanded you not to eat?'" (Genesis 3:11).*

THE TALK: Adam and Eve were comfortable being in God's presence until they disobeyed. Disobedience introduced them to shame for the first time, and they realized they were naked. They had never had any clothes, but now they felt the need to hide their guilt and shame. The problem wasn't their nakedness. The problem was their shame. Sometimes we are also afraid of exposing ourselves before God, but the problem isn't the nakedness of our soul—the problem is our guilt and shame. Satan wants us to hide in shame, afraid to come before God. But God didn't leave Adam and Eve alone in their nakedness. He made them clothes, covering their sin with His grace. And God still covers us. His presence isn't to punish you but to protect you. Draw near to God so He can clothe you in His grace.

Naked and Ashamed:

1. *Realize that it's Satan's job to keep you ashamed.*

2. *Remember that God's presence is not meant to punish you but to protect you.*

3. *Nakedness is only the state of the condition you're in as you wait for God to clothe you.*

THE TAKEAWAY: Draw close to God. He's not coming to scare you; He's coming to clothe you with His grace.

THURSDAY - Relationship Test

THE TEXT: *"And a man lame from birth was being carried, whom they laid daily at the gate of the temple that is called the Beautiful Gate to ask alms of those entering the temple"* (Acts 3:2).

THE TALK: Every day a man who had been lame from birth was brought to beg at the temple gate. He had been crippled all his life. Disability was all he knew. His friends brought him as far as they could take him, but God had other plans for him. When he asked Peter and John for money, they didn't have anything to give him. They gave him what they did have: the power of God. God healed the man, and he entered the temple alongside them, praising God. Sometimes we need to check our relationships. People in our life may mean well, but they can only take us so far. We need people around us who can help usher us into the very presence and power of God. What kind of results do you see from your relationships?

Test Your Relationships:

1. *Are they able to carry you into God's presence?*

2. *Are they helping you progress or leaving you crippled?*

3. *Are they equipping you for possibilities and for praise or for petty pity parties?*

THE TAKEAWAY: Check your relationships. Make sure they lead you to God's presence, power, and praise.

FRIDAY - The Friends You Need

THE TEXT: *"And when Jesus saw their faith, he said to the paralytic 'Son, your sins are forgiven'"* (Mark 2:5).

THE TALK: One day as Jesus was teaching in Capernaum, four friends tried to bring a paralyzed man to Jesus. But the house was so crowded they couldn't even get in the door. The four friends carried the man and his mat up onto the roof, dug a hole in the roof, and lowered him down before Jesus. When Jesus saw their faith, He forgave the man's sins and healed the man. We need friends who are willing to climb walls and rip roofs open to get us to Jesus. And that's also the kind of friend we need to be.

True Friends:

1. *Overcome obstacles to get their friends to Jesus.*

2. *Are willing to step outside the lines and find creative solutions so they can get their friends to Jesus' feet.*

3. *Are filled with faith in what Jesus can do.*

THE TAKEAWAY: Choose friends who can help you get to Jesus.

WEEKEND REFLECTION

"A friend loves at all times, and a brother is born for adversity" (Proverbs 17:17).

FOR REFLECTION: Faithful friends are priceless. True friends aren't just friends when the going is good. They stick with you in hard times, and they point you to God. Who are the stick-with-you friends in your life? Thank God for the gift of friendship, and ask God to help you be a faithful friend.

_____

_____

_____

_____

_____

_____

Week Thirty-Nine

MONDAY - Don't Tap Out

THE TEXT: *"In all this Job did not sin or charge God with wrong" (Job 1:22).*

THE TALK: Job lost everything in a moment. There was a spiritual battle waging that Job knew nothing about, and he was caught in the crossfire. He lost his children. He lost his wealth. He lost his health. His wife urged him to curse God and die. His friends insisted he must have done something wrong. In his frustration, Job said he loathed his very life. Yet he did not sin or accuse God of wrongdoing. Don't tap out when the going gets hard. Your strength is not gone. Hold on till the end, keep doing what is right, and let God deliver you.

Don't Tap Out:

1. *There may be a battle going on you know nothing about.*

2. *What doesn't kill you will make you better.*

3. *Your deliverance is closer than you think.*

THE TAKEAWAY: Don't give up, don't give in, and don't give out. Keep doing what is right, and God will deliver you.

TUESDAY - Expect a Blessing

THE TEXT: *"To grant to all those who mourn in Zion—to give them a beautiful headdress instead of ashes, the oil of gladness instead of mourning, the garment of praise instead of a faint spirit; that they may be called oaks of righteousness, the planting of the Lord, that he may be glorified" (Isaiah 61:3).*

THE TALK: The way things are now is not the way they always have to be. If you are mourning or in pain, distress, or sorrow, know this season will not last forever. Jesus came to bring transformation. He came to rescue the outcast, the prisoner, the broken, and the downtrodden and set them free. He gives us gladness for our mourning, praise in place of our weakness, and the beauty of His glory in place of the bitter ashes of our sin. Jesus brings transformation wherever He goes, and He's coming to you. Are you ready?

The Blessed Transformation:

1. *Jesus takes your mourning, ashes, and despair and replaces them with joy, beauty, and praise.*

2. *The year of the Lord's favor is now. Your freedom is near.*

3. *He has a double portion of blessings for you. Expect your transformation.*

THE TAKEAWAY: Put on the praise equal to the blessing you expect. Today is your day of salvation.

WEDNESDAY - No Looking Back

THE TEXT: *"But Lot's wife, behind him, looked back, and she became a pillar of salt"* (Genesis 19:26).

THE TALK: As Lot and his family escaped Sodom, the angels warned them not to look back at the destruction. But Lot's wife looked back, and she became a pillar of salt.

We are not made to look behind us. Owls can turn their heads 270 degrees so they can see almost all the way around. We can't do that. You were not built to turn around, so why are you trying to see what's behind you? The past has passed. It's gone. You can't change it, but you can learn from it. It's time to get over the pain of your past and celebrate that you made it through. Stop looking behind and start looking ahead. Who does God want you to be?

Three Reminders about the Past:

1. *You are not built to turn around.*

2. *You know where you've been. Why are you trying to see where you went?*

3. *You passed it by. Celebrate that you made it through.*

THE TAKEAWAY: Get the past out of your sightline and focus on what God has in store for you up ahead.

THURSDAY – The Power of a Second Chance

THE TEXT: *"And falling to the ground he heard a voice saying to him, 'Saul, Saul, why are you persecuting me?'" (Acts 9:4).*

THE TALK: God gives second chances. We all need them. And Saul—Saul needed them more than most. Saul was the most dangerous kind of wrong there is: a person who's wrong, thinks he's right, and believes he's serving God in the process. A dedicated, educated Jew, Saul was convinced that it was blasphemy to accept Jesus as the Messiah. He held the cloaks for the men who stoned the first martyr to death. And zealous in his persecution of Christians, Saul got permission to arrest men and women alike. But God stopped him in his tracks on the way to Damascus. He met Jesus there in the middle of the dusty road, and that encounter with Jesus changed everything. Saul, persecutor of the church, became Paul, the greatest evangelist in Christian history. Paul never stopped being thankful for God's gracious gift of a new beginning.

The Power of a Second Chance:

1. *Second chances give you the opportunity to correct your wrong.*

2. *Second chances allow you to project God's forgiveness.*

3. *Second chances protect your future so you can fulfill your destiny.*

THE TAKEAWAY: Take advantage of your second chance.

FRIDAY - Part of the Plan

THE TEXT: *"[They] plotted together to arrest Jesus by stealth and kill him"* (Matthew 26:4).

THE TALK: Tuesday of Passover Week was a day for praise. But Caiaphas and the other Jewish leaders used the day to plot against Jesus and plan for His demise. Sometimes people do the same thing to us, hatching plots and plans to bring us down. But don't worry. Their worst plots are all part of the plan. God is in control of your destiny, and no human scheme can alter His plans for you. Trust Him.

When People Plot:

1. *Don't worry about their plans because their plans will fail.*

2. *They may plan, but God's purpose will prevail.*

3. *If killing you is part of the plan, God will resurrect you.*

THE TAKEAWAY: Your enemies' plans are all part of God's plan to give you the victory.

WEEKEND REFLECTION

"Why do the nations rage and the peoples plot in vain? . . . He who sits in the heavens laughs; the Lord holds them in derision" (Psalm 2:1, 4).

FOR REFLECTION: The leaders of the nations may plot and scheme, but none of their plans can alter the course of our Almighty God. God's sovereignty is unalterable. How does your knowledge of God's absolute power encourage you when the world seems to spin out of control? Ask God to increase your faith in His power to control your destiny.

_____

_____

_____

_____

_____

_____

_____

_____

_____

_____

_____

_____

_____

_____

_____

☀

DEVOTIONS FOR

Fall

Week Forty

MONDAY - Sing Your Song

THE TEXT: *"And Saul was very angry, and this saying displeased him. He said, 'They have ascribed to David ten thousands, and to me they have ascribed thousands, and what more can he have but the kingdom?'" (1 Samuel 18:8).*

THE TALK: After David killed Goliath, his popularity soared. The women sang about David's victory and the great number of the enemy he had killed. But they gave David credit for killing more men than King Saul, and Saul became jealous. The next day a spirit possessed Saul and he attempted to kill David. From then on, Saul regarded David as an enemy.

God has given you a song to sing. Sing it loudly. No one else can sing your song for you, and you can't sing anybody else's song for them. And don't compare your song to anyone else's. Comparison is a tool of the devil. Saul's foolish jealousy made him vulnerable to the evil spirit that prompted him to attempt to murder David. Don't give Satan any room to play his opportunistic games. Stop worrying about what everyone else is singing or what they think about your song. You've got a song to sing. Sing it for your audience of one.

Singing Your Song:

1. *God gives everyone a song.*

2. *Reject comparison and jealousy so Satan doesn't get a foothold in your life.*

3. *Sing the song God gave you.*

THE TAKEAWAY: The melody, harmony, and lyrics of your song can only be sung by you. Sing it!

TUESDAY - Celebrate Favor

THE TEXT: *"And Jonathan stripped himself of the robe that was on him and gave it to David, and his armor, and even his sword and his bow and his belt"* (1 Samuel 18:4).

THE TALK: While Saul was threatened by God's favor toward David, Jonathan celebrated it. Jonathan was Saul's son and heir, but God had chosen David to replace Saul as king. Jonathan could have followed Saul down the pathway of jealousy and anger, but instead he chose to make a covenant with David. The two warriors became close friends. Jonathan gave David his robe, armor, and weapons as a sign of the covenant between them. Since the robe Jonathan gave David was likely his royal robe, the gift may have meant Jonathan both recognized and accepted that David would be the next king. Like Jonathan, we don't have to be threatened by other people's success. Celebrate God's favor on those around you. If you honor them, God will honor you.

Celebrating Favor:

1. *Honor those whom God honors.*

2. *Develop relationships with people whom God shows favor.*

3. *Trust that as God honors them, He will also honor you.*

THE TAKEAWAY: Celebrate with those around you when God shows them favor. He will also honor you.

WEDNESDAY - Don't Take a Sick Day

THE TEXT: *"This is the day that the Lord has made; let us rejoice and be glad in it"* (Psalm 118:24).

THE TALK: Some mornings feel tougher than others. You don't want to get up. You can't bear the thought of facing the same crises and conflicts all over again. It's tempting to just take a pass. Call in sick. Call it off. Let someone else do it for a change. But this day—every day—even the hard days—is a day God has made. Rejoice and be glad in it! This day is a gift and an opportunity. God is present in your day, so you need to be present too. Show up so God can show off in you.

Three Reasons to Show Up:

1. *You may be sick and tired, but you aren't sick. The joy of the Lord is your strength, so rejoice!*

2. *God has given you the gift of this day. Don't reject it.*

3. *You have to show up so God can show off in you. Be His witness.*

THE TAKEAWAY: Don't call in sick. Show up. Rejoice. Thank God for the gift of the day, and see what He wants to do.

THURSDAY - Fans, Followers, and Finishers

THE TEXT: *"And the crowds that went before him and that followed him were shouting, 'Hosanna to the Son of David! Blessed is he who comes in the name of the Lord! Hosanna in the highest!'"* (Matthew 21:9).

THE TALK: On the Sunday before Passover Jesus rode into Jerusalem. The crowds cheered Him. They lined the road with their own coats so the donkey's hooves wouldn't touch the ground. They waved palm branches and shouted as they welcomed Jesus into town. But crowds are fickle. The same crowd that shouted "Hosanna" on Sunday shouted "Crucify" on Friday. Of those that accompanied Him down the road that Sunday, only a handful were willing to stand in the shadow of the cross. What kind of a Jesus-follower will you be?

Three Types of Followers:

1. *Fans are both fanatical and fickle, cheering when you win and turning on you when you lose.*

2. *Followers are along for the ride, but they leave when the going gets tough.*

3. *Finishers stay with Jesus all the way and get to witness the resurrection.*

THE TAKEAWAY: You can be a fan, a follower, or a finisher. Choose the kind of Jesus- follower you will be.

FRIDAY - Show Up Anyway

THE TEXT: *"When the Sabbath was past, Mary Magdalene, Mary the mother of Jesus, and Salome bought spices so that they might go and anoint him"* (Mark 16:1).

THE TALK: The three women thought they were going to a funeral. Jesus was dead. They had seen Him die. They had seen Joseph hastily prepare His body for burial and lay Him in the tomb. And now they were doing the last thing they thought they could do for the teacher they had loved: prepare His body for the grave. They got up early that Sunday morning, got their spices, and went to the tomb. They showed up. And because they showed up, they got to be witnesses to the resurrection. When you think all hope is gone, show up anyway. If you show up, you might get to see a miracle. But you won't know unless you're there.

Three Reasons to Show Up:

1. *Show up because it's not over until Jesus says it's done.*

2. *Show up, because who else is going to save you but Jesus?*

3. *Show up because Jesus is coming. Don't miss the miracle.*

THE TAKEAWAY: Even when your hope is crushed, show up anyway. It's the only way to see the miracle.

WEEKEND REFLECTION

"Trust in him at all times, O people. Pour out your heart before him. God is a refuge for us" (Psalm 62:8).

FOR REFLECTION: Trust in God at all times. *All times.* When things are going well. When they aren't. When you're happy, sad, glad, mad or somewhere in between. Trust God and pour out your heart before Him because God is your refuge. In what areas of your life have you experienced the benefits of trust? In what areas do you need to trust Him more? Pour out your heart to God and ask Him to increase your trust in Him.

Week Forty-One

MONDAY - Family Draft

THE TEXT: *"But when his brothers saw that their father loved him more than all his brothers, they hated him and could not speak peacefully to him"* (Genesis 37:4).

THE TALK: When players are drafted into the NFL they can't choose their team. They have to play for the team that drafts them. In the same way, we can't choose our families. We have to play the game of life with the family God gives us. If Joseph could have chosen, he might have picked a different family situation. Joseph's father, Jacob, had twelve sons by four different women. The situation was ripe for conflict, but Jacob made it worse by choosing Joseph as his favorite son. Jacob's overt favoritism caused Joseph's brothers to hate him. Eventually they faked his death and sold him into slavery. But God remained the author of Joseph's story. God took Joseph from slavery to the second highest position in the land of Egypt, and God placed Joseph in a position where he could save his family. Joseph was his family's most valuable player and he changed the trajectory of his family's history. We can't choose our families, but we can help them win.

Winning with Your Family:

1. *You can't pick your family. God chose them for you.*

2. *Rely on God to help with the family He gave you.*

3. *You have to play the game of life with the family team you're on.*

4. *One player—or one family member—can make a difference.*

THE TAKEAWAY: You are God's number one draft pick. Help your family team win.

TUESDAY - Child's Play

THE TEXT: *"Like arrows in the hand of a warrior are the children of one's youth. Blessed is the man who fills his quiver with them!" (Psalm 127:4-5).*

THE TALK: Children are a gift from God. The Bible also tells us they are weapons of warfare. We nurture our children in the Lord so we can release them into the world as agents of God's kingdom, ready to penetrate the forces of darkness with gospel light. We spend time helping our children pursue their interests and equipping them for a future career. We also need to prepare them for life in the kingdom of God. Point your children to Jesus. Teach them to replicate, represent, and reproduce kingdom principles so they are ready to be shot into the heart of the enemy and take him down. Help them understand the spiritual battle we face and equip them to fight it well. Guide them as they develop Christ-like character and learn to live by the Spirit's power. Your children will have to fight. Give them the tools they need for victory.

How to Weaponize Your Family:

1. *Lead your children to Christ.*

2. *Instill kingdom principles in them.*

3. *Equip them for the spiritual battle they will face.*

THE TAKEAWAY: Parenting is not child's play. Prepare your children for victory.

WEDNESDAY - Baby Daddy Drama

THE TEXT: *"So God created man in his own image . . . And God blessed them. And God said to them, 'Be fruitful and multiply and fill the earth and subdue it'" (Genesis 1:26-27).*

THE TALK: Do you ever wonder why we have so much baby daddy and baby mama drama? We have misunderstood the power of the seed. Reproduction is a powerful privilege with a purpose given by God. It's not a casual activity of pleasure or entertainment for a one-night stand. God intended for a man and woman made in His image to enter into the covenant bond of marriage. The marriage covenant provides the context in which we are to produce children in order to fill the earth and bring creation under God's command. Harness your seed for its God-intended purpose.

The Power of Your Seed:

1. Your seed is a weapon of spiritual warfare (Psalm 127:4).

2. Your seed is a legacy.

3. Your seed is the salt that seasons the earth.

THE TAKEAWAY: Don't sell your seed short. Put a ring on it before you plant.

THURSDAY - The Male Factor

THE TEXT: *"So God created man in his own image" (Genesis 1:27).*

THE TALK: Men, it's time to stand up. You are created in the image of God, made to look like your Father. As images of God, you have the responsibility of representing His power and authority to the world. You are gifted with the task of bringing the world under God's rightful dominion, and God has delegated to you the grace and power you need to do it.

You carry the seeds of the kingdom with you. Be careful where you plant them, and care for the gardens you plant. God has given you a job. Do it well.

Planting the Seed:

1. You carry the seeds of the kingdom with you.

2. Be mindful of the garden where you choose to plant.

3. Care for the seed. Tend the garden God has given you.

THE TAKEAWAY: The male factor is a God idea, not a man idea.

FRIDAY - Precious Treasure

THE TEXT: "An excellent wife who can find? She is far more precious than jewels" (Proverbs 31:10).

THE TALK: Ladies, God considers you a priceless treasure. But that doesn't mean you are meant to be hidden away in a jewel box. The phrase used in Proverbs 31:10 to describe an "excellent wife" can also mean "woman of valor." The Old Testament uses the same words to describe valiant and mighty warriors. Being a woman of excellence is more than matching socks and getting dinner on the table on time. Being a woman of excellence means having the wisdom to fight for your family, showing them how to live with conviction and courage in an unrighteous world. Don't be afraid to take a stand—and don't let anyone treat you as less than you are. God says you are priceless.

Women of Excellence:

1. Know how to live wisely in a foolish world.

2. Model how to live with courage and conviction.

3. Are more valuable than precious jewels.

THE TAKEAWAY: Wise and courageous women are worth more than priceless jewels. Live like the treasure you are.

WEEKEND REFLECTION

"Put off your old self, which belongs to your former manner of life and is corrupt through deceitful desires, and to be renewed in the spirit of your minds, and to put on the new self, created after the likeness of God in true righteousness and holiness" (Ephesians 4:22-24).

FOR REFLECTION: When you followed Christ, God gave you a new self—a self no longer corrupted by sin and created to reflect God's holy and righteous character. But every morning you choose which self to put on. Which self have you put on this week? Have you dressed yourself in holiness and righteousness or in your old sinful rags? Ask God to help you lay aside your old self and put on your new self, clothed in righteousness and truth.

_____

_____

_____

_____

_____

_____

_____

_____

_____

Week Forty-Two

MONDAY - Stop Your Pity Party

THE TEXT: *"But he himself went a day's journey into the wilderness and came and sat down under a broom tree. And he asked that he might die, saying 'It is enough; now O Lord, take away my life, for I am no better than my fathers'"* (1 Kings 19:4).

THE TALK: Elijah was physically, mentally, and spiritually exhausted. After he defeated the prophets of Baal, Queen Jezebel threatened his life and he fled into the wilderness. Completely spent, the prophet sat under a broom bush and asked God to take his life. Maybe you've been there—so worn down and beat up that you're ready for the Lord to take you home. But there's a way out of the pit for you just as there was for Elijah. Elijah fell asleep as he sat under the bush, and an angel came and brought him food. The angel's food strengthened Elijah enough for him to finish his forty-day journey to the place he had planned to meet with God. When you're exhausted and ready to quit, take time to rest and care for yourself. Resting and feeding our bodies can be the most spiritual thing we do. After you've rested, get ready to step back into the fight. As you stand up to finish your journey, remember what has brought you this far. Listen for God's voice. He's not done with you yet.

Get Out of the Pit:

1. *Take time to rest and nourish your body.*

2. *Step up and get back into the fight.*

3. *Get to a place you can meet with God and listen for His voice.*

THE TAKEAWAY: Stay with God. He's not done with you yet.

TUESDAY – Speak Up God, I Can't Hear You

THE TEXT: *"And after the earthquake a fire, but the Lord was not in the fire. And after the fire the sound of a low whisper"* (1 Kings 19:12).

THE TALK: Have you ever needed to hear from God, but it seems like He's quit talking? That was how Elijah felt. He had dramatically defeated the prophets of Baal at Mount Carmel, but Jezebel's threat against his life sent him running for the hills. Elijah believed he was alone. He looked for God's voice in the whirlwind. He looked for God's voice in the earthquake. He looked for God's voice in the fire. But there was no answer. God's voice finally came to Elijah in a quiet and gentle whisper. Sometimes when we need to hear from God, we need to stop looking and start listening. God is talking. Are you listening for Him?

How to Listen to God:

1. *Stop looking for answers and start listening to God's voice.*

2. *Learn God's voice for you and your situation.*

3. *Learn the lessons God teaches in the waiting.*

THE TAKEAWAY: You are not alone. God is talking. Are you prepared to listen?

WEDNESDAY – Don't Self Sabotage

THE TEXT: *"I, even I only am left, and they seek my life, to take it away"* (1 Kings 19:14).

THE TALK: Elijah was at rock bottom. He believed he was the only one of God's prophets left, and he feared his enemy. He was ready to throw in the towel. But God wasn't done with Elijah yet. He still had work to do. Elijah had fallen into a destructive cycle. Instead of conquering his thoughts, Elijah had let his negative thoughts conquer him. Instead of positioning himself for victory, Elijah had run away and positioned himself for defeat. And he had looked for God in the spectacle instead of listening for Him in the silence. Elijah had gotten in the way of his own success. Don't self-sabotage your success. God is for you.

Three Ways to Avoid Self-Sabotage:

1. Conquer your thoughts before they conquer you.

2. Position yourself for victory, not defeat.

3. Listen for God's voice in the silence.

THE TAKEAWAY: God is for you and wants to bring you success. Don't self-sabotage God's plans for you.

THURSDAY - A Penny for Your Thoughts

THE TEXT: *"Whatever is true, whatever is honorable, whatever is just, whatever is pure, whatever is lovely, whatever is commendable, if there is any excellence, if there is anything worthy of praise, think about these things" (Philippians 4:8).*

THE TALK: Paul wrote the book of Philippians from a Roman prison, but he chose to set his thoughts on freedom. Paul knew the enemy always attacks your mind first. If Satan can worm his way into your thoughts, the rest is easy. Guard your thoughts by intentionally filling your mind with what is good, true and pure. Seek out what is just, lovely, and commendable. Don't waste time fretting over the mistakes of the past. Think about what God is going to do tomorrow. Dwell on God's promises and words, and your thinking will be transformed. Your thoughts determine your future.

Think on These Things:

1. *Yesterday-focused thinking costs too much and pays too little.*

2. *Focus your thoughts on what God is doing today and will do tomorrow.*

3. *Transform and renew your mind by meditating on God's promise and words.*

THE TAKEAWAY: Your thoughts are worth more than a penny. Your thoughts are the price of your future.

FRIDAY - A Glorious Inheritance

THE TEXT: *"That you may know . . . the riches of his glorious inheritance in the saints, and what is the immeasurable greatness of his power toward us who believe" (Ephesians 1:18-19).*

THE TALK: God is not stingy in His gifts to His people. In Christ Jesus we have an inheritance greater and more glorious than this world has ever seen. The power He displays toward us is immeasurable. The love He gives us defies description. And all authority belongs to Christ Jesus, who has delegates His power and authority to us that we may glorify Him. You are not a nobody. You are rich in faith and you bring the power of heaven with you when you walk into the room. You have authority to command situations and the power to transform them. Christ has given you the fullness of His blessing. Use it for Him.

Your Inheritance:

1. *God has showered the blessings of heaven on you.*

2. *God has delegated His authority to you.*

3. *God demonstrates His power through you.*

THE TAKEAWAY: God shares His blessing, power, and authority with you. Use your inheritance well.

WEEKEND REFLECTION

"For God gave us a spirit not of fear but of power and love and self-control" (2 Timothy 1:7)

FOR REFLECTION: Fear is not of God. God didn't give you a spirit of fear. He gave you a spirit that exercises and demonstrates power, love, and self-control. When you are afraid, how can relying on God's power give you courage? How can love and self-control be the answer to fear? Ask God to help you overcome fear and live in the powerful, loving, and disciplined spirit He has given you.

Week Forty-Three

MONDAY - Christ Crossed Out Our Curse

THE TEXT: *"Christ redeemed us from the curse of the law by becoming a curse for us—for it is written, 'Cursed is everyone who is hanged on a tree'"* (Galatians 3:13).

THE TALK: Before we came to Christ, we all lived under a curse. Apart from Christ we were bound to follow the law, powerless to obey it, and doomed to suffer the consequences of our disobedience. But Christ canceled our curse by becoming the curse for us. The law declared that anyone hung on a cross was under God's curse. By willingly going to the cross, Jesus became the curse in order to break it. Christ alone was sinless; He alone had fully kept the law and did not deserve its punishment. He chose to take death upon himself, crossing out our sin and releasing grace. He redeemed us from all curses—generational curses, curses of disobedience, and the curse of sin and death. Christ broke the curse and offered us blessing in its place.

Christ Broke the Curse:

1. *Christ cursed the curse, becoming the curse that He might break it.*

2. *Christ crossed out our sin and released grace.*

3. *Christ redeemed us from all curses and secured our salvation.*

THE TAKEAWAY: Because Christ has broken the curse, no curse can control you. Walk in freedom.

TUESDAY - Give Him Everything

THE TEXT: *"Now when Jesus was at Bethany in the home of Simon the leper, a woman came up to him with an alabaster flask of very expensive ointment, and she poured it on his head as he reclined at table" (Matthew 26:6-7).*

THE TALK: In the last days before Jesus gave His life for us, a woman gave up her most valuable possession for Him. She found Jesus at the home of Simon the leper. She had an alabaster flask of expensive ointment, and she poured it out upon Jesus' head as an offering of worship. The disciples called it a waste, saying that the valuable perfume could have been sold and the money given to the poor, but Jesus accepted her sacrifice. She understood what the disciples did not: Jesus' moment of sacrifice was coming. She had anointed Him for His burial. Though she is not named in this passage, we remember her story. She gave everything and gained a legacy.

Are you willing to give Jesus that which is most precious to you? What hidden treasures have you stored away? Maybe it's the money in your bank account or a treasured heirloom. Or maybe it's something less tangible. A talent you've refused to surrender. Hours in the week you fiercely guard. Or maybe it's your family—God can do with you what He wants, but He'd better not call your children to a place you can't follow. Whatever it is, pour it all out for Jesus. Sacrifice it for Him. Others may say it's a waste, but worship is never wasted. Give Him everything, and gain a legacy.

Giving Everything:

1. *Search for Jesus wherever He can be found.*

2. *Sacrifice for Jesus and give Him everything.*

3. *Serve Jesus and leave a legacy.*

THE TAKEAWAY: When you give Jesus everything in worship, He gives you a legacy.

WEDNESDAY - Runaway Emotions, Part 1

THE TEXT: *"But Jonah rose to flee to Tarshish from the presence of the Lord" (Jonah 1:3).*

THE TALK: Jonah ran away from God. God told him to go preach to Nineveh, the home of some of Israel's greatest enemies. Jonah couldn't bear the thought of the people of Nineveh repenting and receiving God's mercy, so he got on a boat and went the opposite direction. It took being swallowed by a fish to get Jonah on the right track. But though he grudgingly followed God's command, he didn't embrace God's heart. He was angry that God showed mercy. Jonah let his emotions get in the way of his obedience. Like Jonah, we must be careful of letting our emotions run our lives. Following your emotions can wreck your relationships and ruin your destiny. Put God in charge of your emotions so they don't run away with you.

The Danger of Runaway Emotions:

1. Runaway emotions can reroute your life.

2. Runaway emotions can wreck your relationships.

3. Runaway emotions can ruin your destiny.

THE TAKEAWAY: Rein in your emotions. Follow God, not your feelings.

THURSDAY - Runaway Emotions, Part 2

THE TEXT: *"Know this, my beloved brothers: let every person be quick to hear, slow to speak, slow to anger; for the anger of man does not produce the righteousness of God" (James 1:19-20).*

THE TALK: We need to run our emotions so our emotions don't run away with us. Self-control is a fruit of the Spirit. As we grow in our relationship with God, we should also grow in our ability to master our emotions. Developing our listening skills is an important action step in learning to rein in our emotions. Too often we aren't really listening to what someone is saying because we're too busy planning what we're going to say in response. Instead of giving them a piece of your mind, make sure you've understood what they're really saying. Be quick to listen and slow to speak. Repeat back what you think you've heard. Often taking time to truly listen cools our anger before it starts.

Listen Well:

1. *Give the person talking your full attention.*

2. *Repeat back to them what you think you've heard.*

3. *Let them correct any misunderstandings.*

4. *Wait to respond until you've heard them out.*

THE TAKEAWAY: Taking time to listen before we speak can cool our anger and rein in our emotions. Learn to listen well.

FRIDAY - Runaway Emotions Part 3

THE TEXT: *"And Peter took him aside and began to rebuke him, saying, 'Far be it from you, Lord! This shall never happen to you'"* (Matthew 16:22).

THE TALK: When Jesus began to tell His disciples about His death and resurrection, the disciples rejected it. Peter took Jesus aside and dared to argue with Him. How could the Messiah die? Peter's response stemmed from a desire to control the situation. He feared what he didn't understand. His desire for control was a hindrance to Jesus' true mission: to give himself as a sacrifice for our sins. Our desire for control is a major source of runaway emotions. Fear of losing control can trigger emotions such as anger and anxiety that make us do irrational things. And our need for control can stifle God's calling in the lives of those around us if we refuse to let them pursue their God-given missions and passions. But control is contrary to faith. Faith surrenders control to God and places the future in His hands. All our attempts at control pale in comparison to God's sovereign power. Stop trying to control your life and put God in charge. You can trust Him.

The Danger of Control:

1. *Control issues are incompatible with faith.*

2. *Control issues can restrict your future.*

3. *Control issues can get in the way of your calling and the calling of those around you.*

THE TAKEAWAY: You can't control the course of your life, but God can. Trust Him.

WEEKEND REFLECTION

"Be angry and do not sin. Do not let the sun go down on your anger" (Ephesians 4:26).

FOR REFLECTION: Anger and other strong emotions are not sins, but we can sin in how we handle them. Have you ever let a strong emotion lead you to sin? How can you honor God with your emotions? Ask God to help you control your emotions and remain obedient to Him.

— FALL —

238

Week Forty-Four

MONDAY - Family Drama

THE TEXT: *"But he would not listen to her, and being stronger than she, he violated her and lay with her"* (2 Samuel 13:7).

THE TALK: You may think you have family drama, but for most of us our drama pales in comparison to the drama found in David's family. One of David's sons, Ammon, raped his half-sister Tamar. David knew but did nothing about it. As a result, Absalom, Tamar's brother, vowed to avenge her. Absalom killed Ammon and rebelled against David.

When drama stirs in your family, you can put it to rest. The first step is recognizing the problem and remedying it. David's inaction let the problem fester and grow. Once you've remedied the problem, you need to restore and renew relationships within the family. David never restored his relationship with Absalom, and so Absalom acted against his father to seize the throne. But if drama strikes in your family, don't give up hope. Even with all of his faults and failures, David was still a man after God's own heart. Despite all the drama, David's family tree leads straight to the source of our redemption: Jesus. Don't lose hope. Your family drama can be redeemed.

Ending the Family Drama:

1. *Recognize and remedy the problem.*

2. *Restore and renew your relationships.*

3. *Remember all things work together for good.*

THE TAKEAWAY: Don't let family drama rip you apart. Hold fast to your family and look for the day of redemption.

TUESDAY - Generational Blessings

THE TEXT: *"And he said, 'I am the God of your father, the God of Abraham, the God of Isaac, and the God of Jacob'"* (Exodus 3:6).

THE TALK: When God identified himself to Moses, He identified himself as the God who had led the generations of Israel's founding fathers. God identifies himself with generations because He acts through families' generations. Right now you are walking in blessings you didn't earn— blessings that have come to you because of the prayers and obedience of people in your family line. You can continue the legacy by praying for blessings that will follow after you on your children, grandchildren, and even the great-grandchildren you may never see. God is in it for the long haul. Leave a blessing for future generations.

Leaving a Blessing:

1. *Thank God for the blessings you walk in that you haven't earned.*

2. *Pray for blessings you won't walk in but future generations will.*

3. *Remember that God looks ahead. Consider how you will impact the future of your family tree.*

THE TAKEAWAY: Blessings are a generational thing. Make sure you understand.

WEDNESDAY - Killing Family Goliaths

THE TEXT: *"And Eliab's anger was kindled against David, and he said, 'Why have you come down? And with whom have you left those few sheep in the wilderness? I know your* *presumption and the evil of your heart, for you have come down to see the battle" (1 Samuel 17:28).*

THE TALK: David's older brothers were part of Israel's defense against the Philistines. David's father sent him to check on his brothers and take them some supplies, but when David arrived he discovered that the entire Israelite army was cowering in fear of Goliath. Every day the giant taunted Israel's forces. David couldn't understand why Israel didn't take Goliath up on his challenge. The living God was stronger than any giant. But David's oldest brother heard David's challenge and rebuked him, misunderstanding his confidence in God for immature pride. David's whole family was ready to fight, but fear made them fight among themselves instead of facing the giant together. And yet David's faith in God was enough to defeat the giant and change his family's history. Your faith can be enough to defeat your family Goliaths, too.

Three Types of Giants:

1. *The giant of finances. Money is one of the top sources of family conflict.*

2. *The giant of relationships. Rivalries and misunderstandings lead to conflict in the family.*

3. *The giant of identity. Knowing who you are in the family can help prevent conflict.*

THE TAKEAWAY: When giants taunt your family, fight the giant and not each other.

THURSDAY - How to Kill Giants

THE TEXT: *"This day the Lord will deliver you into my hand, and I will strike you down and cut off your head" (1 Samuel 17:46).*

THE TALK: David faced Goliath with confidence because he knew the Lord had given the giant into his hand. But he had to fight the battle the Lord's way. He couldn't use Saul's armor—it wasn't made for him. He had to face the giant in his own identity. And David was creative, using the weapons he had at hand to bring the Philistine warrior down. In the hands of God, a simple stone and sling are more powerful than a mighty sword. But most importantly, David recognized that the battle wasn't about him but about God. Goliath had taunted the armies of the Living God, and it was in the name of the Lord that David dared stand against the giant. When you face giants, remember no giant is ever bigger than your God.

How to Kill a Giant:

1. *Fight as yourself, not using a borrowed identity.*

2. *Be creative and use the weapons God gives you.*

3. *Stand for God and let Him win the victory for you.*

THE TAKEAWAY: It isn't your size or the size of your giants that will determine the battle—it's the size of your God.

FRIDAY - Refine My Family

THE TEXT: *"Whoever troubles his own household will inherit the wind"* (Proverbs 11:29).

THE TALK: Struggles in your home will blow through the rest of your life like the wind. Don't be the one who causes trouble in your family. Be the one who refines it. Refine your relationships, building strong connections between husband and wife, parents and children, singles and the rest of your extended family. Refine your resources, learning to tell your money what to do so you can leave an inheritance for your children's children. And refine your family's future by leaving a spiritual legacy for the generations to come.

Three Things to Refine:

1. *Refine your family relationships.*

2. *Refine your family resources.*

3. *Refine your family's future.*

THE TAKEAWAY: Let God refine your family so you can produce fruit.

WEEKEND REFLECTION

"Is this not the fast that I choose, to loose the bonds of wickedness, to undo the straps of the yoke, to let the oppressed go free, and to break every yoke?" (Isaiah 58:6).

FOR REFLECTION: God wants His people to be involved in bringing justice. Our religion is worthless if we are not involved in bringing freedom to the oppressed and breaking the yokes that hold them captive. What forces of oppression do you see at work in your world? How can you be a part of breaking those yokes and setting people free? Ask God to give you the opportunity to work for justice and freedom.

Week Forty-Five

MONDAY - The Nathan Effect

THE TEXT: *"And the Lord sent Nathan to David"* (2 Samuel 12:1).

THE TALK: David was a great king, but he also sinned greatly. He committed adultery and sent a man to his death to cover it up. He thought he had gotten away with it, but God was not deceived. God sent the prophet Nathan to confront David with his sin. Nathan boldly challenged David about his sin. Overcome with grief, David repented, and Nathan gave David God's message of judgment and restoration.

We need people in our lives like Nathan who can confront us with our sin and point us to restoration. We need people who are willing to risk our anger to speak hard truths and people whom we trust to speak God's message into our lives. Their goal is not to destroy us but to point us to our destiny. Who are the Nathans in your life, and who can you be a Nathan to?

Friends Like Nathan:

1. *Can speak hard truths in a way that helps us accept them.*

2. *Confront us with the truth and point us to repentance.*

3. *Desire to see us reach our destiny.*

THE TAKEAWAY: Find friends who are willing to speak truth into your life, leading you to repentance and pointing you to your destiny.

TUESDAY - Not Alone

THE TEXT: *"Then the Lord God said, 'It is not good that the man should be alone; I will make him a helper fit for him'"* (Genesis 2:18).

THE TALK: The story of creation ends the account of what God did each day with a familiar refrain: "And God saw that it was good." Then suddenly the pattern changes: God saw something that was not good. It was not good for the man to be alone. God met the man's need by creating woman. It is not good for us to be alone, either. We were created for community and relationship. We need people around us, and God still meets that need for us just as He did for Adam. Ask God to bring people into your life. Ask for a Paul who challenges you and calls you to a higher level of living. Ask for a Timothy who you can teach and disciple. And ask for a Barnabas, someone to walk by your side and encourage you. God has made you for greatness, but you can't do it alone.

Three People You Need in Your Life:

1. *A Paul who mentors and challenges you.*

2. *A Timothy who you are teaching and discipling.*

3. *A Barnabas who walks beside you and encourages you.*

THE TAKEAWAY: You were not made to be alone. Ask God to surround you with people who will accompany you on your path to greatness.

WEDNESDAY - It's Your Time

THE TEXT: *"For everything there is a season, and a time for every matter under heaven"* (Ecclesiastes 3:1).

THE TALK: Every season has a purpose. Spring is the time for planting, summer is a time for growth, and fall is a time for harvest. Even in winter as the earth lies quiet and dormant, growth is still happening underground as roots spread and seeds germinate, preparing for the new birth of spring. Every season of your life has a purpose as well. Some seasons are times of growth. Other seasons are times of fruitful harvest. And some seasons are times of rest, letting old things die so new growth can take its place. What season are you in?

Finding the Season:

1. *Figure out the season you are in.*

2. *Make sure your actions match your season.*

3. *Remember that seasons change. Your current season won't last forever.*

THE TAKEAWAY: Every season has a purpose. Discover the purpose of your season.

THURSDAY - Turn Your Power On

THE TEXT: *"For my power is made perfect in weakness" (2 Corinthians 12:9).*

THE TALK: Our weaknesses are the vehicles of God's power. God delights in transformation. He makes kings out of shepherd boys and turns cowering farmers into mighty warriors. And He chooses our weaknesses to display His strength. Refusing to admit our need only blocks the flow of God's power in our lives. His power doesn't turn on till we turn ours off. Our world despises and mocks weakness, but it is when we are most vulnerable that God is best able to use us. We've got to get ourselves out of the way so His power can flow in. Boast in your weaknesses, for they are the windows through which God displays His strength in you.

Three Things About Power:

1. *God's power turns on when yours turns off.*

2. *You access God's power through fervent prayer.*

3. *Remain in a state of vulnerability so God can prove His strength.*

THE TAKEAWAY: Don't be ashamed of weakness. Your weakness is how God displays His strength in you.

FRIDAY - The Job Effect

THE TEXT: *"And the Lord said to Satan, 'Have you considered my servant Job, that there is none like him on the earth; a blameless and upright man, who fears God and turns away from evil?'" (Job 1:8).*

THE TALK: Satan's name means "accuser," and that's what Satan does: accuse us before the Father. But God doesn't give Satan's accusations any room. God endorses you. He is for you. He celebrates your faithfulness and your endurance. He is cheering you on to victory, and He will not let you fail. Don't let Satan's accusations get you down. God accepts you.

How God Feels About You:

1. *God endorses you.*

2. *God is cheering for you.*

3. *God won't let you fail.*

THE TAKEAWAY: Accept what God says about you and reject everything else.

❦

WEEKEND REFLECTION

"Who is to condemn? Christ Jesus is the one who died—more than that, who was raised—who is at the right hand of God, who indeed is interceding for us" (Romans 8:34).

FOR REFLECTION: Jesus himself intercedes for us before the Father. Who can condemn us if Christ is for us? Don't listen to the voices of condemnation and judgment. Listen to Jesus, who pleads on your behalf. What does God say about you? How can listening to God's voice help you silence accusations and condemnation? Ask God to remind you who He says you are.

_____

_____

_____

_____

_____

_____

_____

_____

_____

_____

_____

_____

_____

Week Forty-Six

MONDAY - Sheep but not Sheepish

THE TEXT: *"Behold, I am sending you out as sheep in the midst of wolves, so be wise as serpents and innocent as doves" (Matthew 10:16).*

THE TALK: Jesus' disciples had watched Him do ministry. Now He was sending them out to practice, heal, and share the good news of God's kingdom. But it was risky. Jesus had faced opposition. His disciples would too. And so Jesus warned them to be both innocent and wise—refusing to participate in evil, but wise enough to recognize it when they saw it. Like the disciples, we must accept that ministry comes with risks. But Jesus didn't die to make us safe. He died to make us dangerous to the devil. When you threaten Satan's dominion, he fights back. Be prepared, but don't be afraid. Jesus promises you the victory.

Innocent and Wise:

1. *As you go, stay shrewd, smart, wise, and creative.*

2. *Stay vigilant, prayerful, and politically engaged.*

3. *Take out the enemy every chance you get.*

THE TAKEAWAY: Jesus died to make you dangerous, and He has given you the victory. Act like the warrior you are.

TUESDAY - Take the Fight to the Devil

THE TEXT: *"On this rock I will build my church, and the gates of hell shall not prevail against it" (Matthew 16:18).*

THE TALK: When the world gets hostile, too often Christians want to retreat to our holy huddles. But you can't win by only playing a defensive game. Jesus wants us to go on offense. And He has promised that when we take the fight to the devil, we will win. The gates of hell will not stand against Christ's church. The church has the power to storm hell itself to set the captives free. Look around you. Where are the places in the community that Satan is holding ground? Who are the men, women, and children trapped in his captivity? Go get them. Satan has no right to that turf, so take the fight to him. Jesus has already promised you will win.

Taking the Fight to the Devil:

1. *Look around. Who is Satan holding captive in your community?*

2. *Get your armor on. Cover your mission in prayer.*

3. *Go. Fight Satan at the very gates of hell. They won't stand against you.*

THE TAKEAWAY: Storm the gates of hell to set Satan's captives free. Jesus has promised you the victory.

WEDNESDAY - Being Salt

THE TEXT: *"You are the salt of the earth, but if salt has lost its taste, how shall its saltiness be restored? It is no longer good for anything except to be thrown out and trampled under people's feet" (Matthew 5:13).*

THE TALK: Salt is distinctive. It preserves food and makes it more palatable. You can tell when food needs salt. But if salt somehow loses its saltiness and flavor, it's useless. As followers of Christ, we need to maintain our distinctive difference in the world, particularly as our nation wrestles with racism and bigotry. The voices of hate are loud, but we have a better story to tell. Our story is that God created all nations from one man, and sent one man—Jesus—to redeem us all. God has gathered for himself a people from every nation, tribe, and tongue and united us in worship of His name. We are equal. We are one. And we are redeemed. Victory and justice will come as we tell our story.

Tell Our Story:

1. *Racism is contrary to the gospel.*

2. *Share what the Bible has to say about equality, reconciliation, and justice.*

3. *Paint a picture of the future God wants for His people.*

THE TAKEAWAY: Be distinctively different and tell a better story: the gospel story.

THURSDAY - Being Light

THE TEXT: *"Nor do people light a lamp and put it under a basket, but on a stand, and it gives light to all in the house"* (Matthew 5:15).

THE TALK: Lights aren't meant to be hidden. They are meant to shine. And in the same way, Christians are not meant to hide behind stained glass windows. We are meant to be lights in our dark world. Too often we are afraid to take positions because we don't want to start conflict or because we're trying to keep peace. But being the voices for justice and equality we are meant to be requires us to speak. There is plenty of evil in our world. Don't be afraid to stand against it. Educate yourself. Advocate your position, and enlighten others. Let your light shine.

Take a Stand:

1. *Educate yourself about the issue.*

2. Prayerfully take a position.

3. Talk about it with people who don't look like you or who disagree.

THE TAKEAWAY: The church wasn't meant to hide. The church was meant to shine. Don't be afraid to take a stand.

FRIDAY - Shine Before Others

THE TEXT: *"In the same way, let your light shine before others, so that they may see your good works and give glory to your Father who is in heaven" (Matthew 5:16).*

THE TALK: *Shine* is not just a word; it's an action. And if we are to let our light shine where others can see it, we need to take action. The world has enough social justice warrior wannabes who save their boldness for their Twitter feed and Facebook page. Real change requires real action among real people. If we want justice, we've got to put muscle power into it. Don't just say you care about the homeless. Serve them a meal. If you care about the unborn, support adoption and foster care and make sure mothers have what they need to care for their babies. If you want to see an end to racism and inequality, show the world what reconciliation and unity look like. Whatever you do, make sure the people watching know it's all for Jesus. Your good works bring glory to God.

Shine Your Light:

1. Don't just say something; do something.

2. Get involved with the causes that matter to you.

3. Preach Jesus while you do it.

THE TAKEAWAY: Words are not enough. We glorify God by what we do.

WEEKEND REFLECTION

"Your kingdom come, your will be done, on earth as it is in heaven" (Matthew 6:10).

FOR REFLECTION: In heaven, God's will is done perfectly and completely. We are to be about extending God's kingdom influence on earth so that God's will is done here just as it is in heaven. How would your community be different if God's will was done in your hometown? What about your family? Your church? Ask God to make you a part of seeing His kingdom come and His will being done in your world.

_____

_____

_____

_____

_____

_____

_____

_____

_____

_____

_____

_____

_____

Week Forty-Seven

MONDAY - How to Find Your Blessing

THE TEXT: *"Go to the sea and cast a hook and take the first fish that comes up, and when you open its mouth you will find a shekel" (Matthew 17:27).*

THE TALK: Tax collectors confronted Peter about whether or not Jesus paid a certain tax. Jesus told Peter to go catch a fish and that He would find the money to pay the tax in the fish's mouth. The mouth of a fish is not a normal place to find a coin, but sometimes our blessing comes from unexpected places. Instead of deciding ahead of time how your blessing is going to come, trust God to work as He pleases. And when your blessing comes, put it to work. God always blesses you for a purpose.

Finding Your Blessing:

1. *Follow Jesus' orders.*

2. *Look for your blessing in unexpected places.*

3. *Put your blessing to work.*

THE TAKEAWAY: You may find your blessing in unexpected places. Don't miss it.

TUESDAY - The Place of Provision

THE TEXT: *"So Abraham called the name of that place, 'The Lord will provide,' as it is said to this day, 'On the mount of the Lord it will be provided'" (Genesis 22:14).*

THE TALK: Abraham went to the mountain of Moriah in obedience to God's command to go there and sacrifice Isaac on the altar. But God's plan was never for Abraham to sacrifice Isaac; God had always intended to provide a substitute sacrifice to take Isaac's place. As Abraham prepared to sacrifice his son, God told Abraham to stop. Abraham looked up and saw a ram caught by the horns in a nearby thicket. The ram took Isaac's place on the altar just as Jesus took our place on the cross. God provided the sacrifice, and God still provides for our needs. The place of your provision is the place of your need—the place where God is present and where you put your trust in Him. Look up. God's provision is waiting for you.

The Lord Who Provides:

1. The Lord provides for our deepest need.

2. The Lord provides out of the riches of His presence.

3. The Lord provides as we place our trust in Him.

THE TAKEAWAY: Expect God to provide.

WEDNESDAY - The Power of Thank You

THE TEXT: *"Oh give thanks to the Lord, for he is good; for his steadfast love endures forever!" (1 Chronicles 16:34).*

THE TALK: Thankfulness is the appropriate response to God's love for us. Thanksgiving is powerful. It forces us to focus on being grateful for how much we have instead of contemplating how much we want and releases God's blessing in our lives. Just as someone showing us appreciation encourages us to do more for them, our thankfulness encourages God to do more for us. Thankfulness removes any thought that you are taking something or someone for granted. It demonstrates your gratitude for how others have blessed you. Give it a try: thank someone.

The Power of Thankfulness:

1. *Reminds you of what you have and not what you want.*

2. *Releases God's power and blessing in your life.*

3. *Removes any thought of being taken for granted.*

THE TAKEAWAY: Say thank you and release God's power in your life.

THURSDAY - Mind Space

THE TEXT: *"Set your minds on things that are above, not on things that are on earth" (Colossians 3:2).*

THE TALK: Changing your thinking can change your destiny. Thoughts become beliefs, beliefs become words, and words become actions. If we can change the way we think, we can change what we say and what we do. Think of your mind as a vault filled with ideas. Your words are ideas wrapped in letters, and your mouth is the combination that opens the vault. You have to change the content of the vault if you want to change what comes out. And so we have to fix our minds on Christ and things above, not on things of this earth. Let Christ form your mind and transform your desires so you can reach your destiny.

Transform Your Mind Space:

1. *Your ideas will become your reality.*

2. *Transform your ideas by thinking on God's Word.*

3. *Ask God to implant His thoughts and desires in you.*

THE TAKEAWAY: Elevate your mind, and you will elevate your destiny.

FRIDAY - Keep Calm

THE TEXT: *"A fool gives full vent to his spirit, but a wise man quietly holds it back" (Proverbs 29:11).*

THE TALK: Have you noticed how angry people seem to be these days? Listen to the news, talk shows, or even what people post on social media. There's a simmering undercurrent of anger that boils up at the slightest provocation. Men and women of wisdom know how to control their anger. Venting may make you feel good for the moment, but it leaves you open to spiritual attack. Venting also lets everyone know how self-centered and selfish you are; you are angry because you want your way. And anger links you to a spirit of self-destruction. Our anger can't accomplish God's purposes. Control your anger before it leads you to defeat.

The Danger of Venting:

1. *It leaves you open to spiritual attack.*

2. *It reveals your selfishness.*

3. *It links you to self-destruction.*

THE TAKEAWAY: Stay calm. Anything else leads you to defeat.

WEEKEND REFLECTION

"But now you must put them all away: anger, wrath, malice, slander, and obscene talk from your mouth" (Colossians 3:8).

FOR REFLECTION: Some things are not fitting for the Christian. Anger, slander, malice, and obscene talk may once have been part of our lives, but now we need to put them away and embrace Christ's character. What parts of your life do you need to put away? What should you welcome in their place? Ask God to help you put away that which is displeasing to Him so you can embrace His holiness.

Week Forty-Eight

MONDAY - My Shepherd

THE TEXT: *"The Lord is my shepherd; I shall not want"* (Psalm 23:1).

THE TALK: There's a person in every family who takes care of everyone else. Sometimes it's Mom, sometimes it's Dad, sometimes it's a grandparent or even an older sibling. That caretaker is the foundation of the family—the person who keeps track of everything and makes sure it all gets done. When we find ourselves in that caretaker role in our families— at work or at church—it's hard to let someone else take care of you. That's what Jesus does. He is your shepherd. Not just your family's or your friend's shepherd, or the shepherd of the next hurting person you talk to. He is your shepherd, and He cares for your soul.

Jesus is Your Shepherd:

1. Learn to see Jesus as your shepherd who cares for you.

2. Trust your shepherd to meet your needs.

3. Let Him take care of you.

THE TAKEAWAY: Jesus is your shepherd and He wants to take care of you. Let Him.

TUESDAY - He Restores My Soul

THE TEXT: *"He restores my soul..." (Psalm 23:3).*

THE TALK: Have you ever seen people restore classic cars? They take an old, rusted out, beat up hulk with holes in the upholstery and a missing fender and turn it into a thing of beauty. They get the engine purring, give it a new paint job, polish up the chrome, and haunt junk dealers looking for original parts. They take something old and make it new again. In the same way, Jesus restores our souls. Where the world leaves us beat up, wounded, and sore, Jesus makes us new again. He heals our hurts. He erases the stain of our sin. He replaces the parts that are broken. And He does it all so we can serve and glorify Him. Don't give up. Give yourself to Him. He restores your soul.

He Restores My Soul:

1. *He heals my hurts.*

2. *He forgives my sin.*

3. *He repairs my brokenness.*

THE TAKEAWAY: Jesus restores broken souls—even yours.

WEDNESDAY - For His Name's Sake

THE TEXT: *"...He leads me in paths of righteousness for his name's sake" (Psalm 23:3).*

THE TALK: God leads us in paths of righteousness. He will never lead you into temptation or sin. God's ways are always perfect, and He will always lead you into what is holy, good, and right. God leads us not just for our own sake but for His. Righteous living is good for us, but it also brings glory to Him. We are meant to bring glory to God's name by how we live.

For His Name:

1. *Glorify God by what you say.*

2. *Glorify God by what you do.*

3. *Glorify God by living for Him.*

🍁

THE TAKEAWAY: God leads us in paths of righteousness so we can glorify Him.

THURSDAY - Fear No Evil

THE TEXT: "Even though I walk through the valley of the shadow of death, I will fear no evil, for you are with me; your rod and your staff, they comfort me" (Psalm 23:4).

THE TALK: There is no place you can go where God is not. You may be walking a dark path or fighting a battle you think you can't win. But God is with you. Even when death's dark shadow lies across your way, you don't have to be afraid. God is there, and you can find comfort in His protection and His justice. You never walk through the valley alone.

In the Valley:

1. *Remember that you are not alone.*

2. *Keep walking till you get to the other side.*

3. *Don't be afraid. God is there.*

THE TAKEAWAY: No darkness is so great God can't guide you. Don't be afraid. He is there.

FRIDAY - Feasting with Your Enemies

THE TEXT: *"You prepare a table before me in the presence of my enemies; you anoint my head with oil; my cup overflows"* (Psalm 23:5).

THE TALK: Your enemies can't destroy you when God holds your future. People may come against you, but they can't derail your destiny. Stay faithful, stay obedient, and endure. God will elevate you in His time. Your enemies will see it, but they can't stop it. You are the honored guest at God's banquet.

He will anoint you with the power of His Spirit and bless you until your cup overflows. Don't worry when your enemies and adversaries try to plot against you. They won't win. Jesus controls your destiny, and He's setting this up so they will witness it.

God's Banquet:

1. *Your enemies can't derail your destiny.*

2. *You are the honored guest at God's banquet.*

3. *Your enemies will watch as God blesses you.*

THE TAKEAWAY: Your enemies can't derail your destiny. They can only watch it unfold.

WEEKEND REFLECTION

"Surely goodness and mercy shall follow me all the days of my life, and I shall dwell in the house of the Lord forever" (Psalm 23:6).

FOR REFLECTION: Goodness and mercy are the markers of God's presence. Wherever He goes, they follow. And since God is always with you, His goodness and mercy will always follow you. How have you experienced God's goodness and mercy? Ask God to open your eyes to how He is blessing you this week. Celebrate His merciful kindness.

_____

_____

_____

_____

_____

Week Forty-Nine

MONDAY - Root of All Evil

THE TEXT: *"For the love of money is a root of all kinds of evils"* (1 Timothy 6:10).

THE TALK: People sometimes misquote this verse to say that money is the root of all kinds of evil. Money in itself isn't bad. Money lets us buy the things we need and enables us to give so others can have what they need. But loving money can lead us to places we should never go. Loving money can lead us to moral compromise and selfish decisions. It causes us to prioritize gaining stuff instead of gaining Jesus, and it steals our worship. In the end, with money, we can't gain the things that really matter. We aren't meant to love money. We're meant to love Jesus.

When You Love Money:

1. *You compromise to get more of it.*

2. *You make selfish decisions to avoid spending it.*

3. *You worship it instead of Jesus.*

THE TAKEAWAY: Steward your money, but don't love it. You were made to love Jesus.

TUESDAY - Who're You Serving?

THE TEXT: *"No one can serve two masters, for either he will hate the one and love the other, or he will be devoted to the one and despise the other. You cannot serve God and money"* (Matthew 6:24).

THE TALK: Have you ever tried to work two jobs? Sometimes it's necessary to take care of your family, but it's hard to do. You're constantly juggling one schedule at the expense of the other or trying to meet two sets of obligations at the same time. Jesus said we aren't meant to serve two masters. We are meant to serve Him, and Him alone. Serving Jesus and our wallets at the same time doesn't work. Serving Jesus means giving Him everything—even our bank accounts. He may ask you to take a job that pays less so you can spend more time with your family. He may ask you to give in a way that doesn't make sense. Or He may ask you to trust His provision instead of what your brain says is the bottom line. You can't serve Jesus and money. What will you choose?

No Competition:

1. *Jesus demands your exclusive devotion.*

2. *He is Lord over everything—even your wallet.*

3. *Prioritize the faithful decision over the financial advantage.*

THE TAKEAWAY: You can't serve both God and money. Who are you going to serve?

WEDNESDAY - True Abundance

THE TEXT: *"And he said to them, 'Take care, and be on your guard against all covetousness, for one's life does not consist in the abundance of his possessions'" (Luke 12:15).*

THE TALK: There's a story told about a rich man who had worked all his life to amass his wealth. On his deathbed he asked his wife to bury him with all his money. She felt she had to honor his request. Before they closed the casket, she slipped a small package in the coffin. "You didn't really put all his money in there, did you?" her friend asked. "I sure did," the widow said. "I wrote him a check."

We laugh at the man's foolishness, but sometimes we make the same mistake. The amount of stuff you have is not the measure of your success. You can't tell a person's character by the brand of their jeans, and you can't tell how righteous someone is by the kind of car they drive. We need to guard against greed and envy. Our life isn't measured by our possessions. It's measured by our faithfulness to God.

The Truth about Money:

1. *The amount of money you have says nothing about your character.*

2. *The amount of money you have says nothing about your worth.*

3. *The amount of money you have says nothing about your obedience.*

THE TAKEAWAY: True success isn't measured by how much stuff we have. True success is measured by our obedience to God.

THURSDAY - Bring the Whole Tithe

THE TEXT: *"Bring the full tithe into the storehouse, that there may be food in my house. And thereby put me to the test, says the Lord of hosts, if I will not open the windows of heaven for you and pour down for you a blessing until there is no more need" (Malachi 3:10).*

THE TALK: God blesses us as we bless Him. The Jews who returned from exile were suffering because they had withheld their tithes and offerings from God. Because they had withheld their tithe, God had withheld His blessing. God told them to bring the full tithe into the storehouse—the temple—and that

He would unlock His blessings. When we take care of God's house, God takes care of ours. Don't rob God by withholding your offerings. Give freely to God if you want Him to give freely to you.

Bring the Whole Tithe:

1. *God blesses us as we bless Him.*

2. *Don't rob God by withholding tithes and offerings.*

3. *Give freely to God and He will give freely to you.*

THE TAKEAWAY: Take care of God's house and He will take care of yours.

FRIDAY - Giving Cheerfully

THE TEXT: *"Each one must give as he has decided in his heart, not reluctantly or under compulsion, for God loves a cheerful giver" (2 Corinthians 9:7).*

THE TALK: God loves it when we give cheerfully and freely to Him. You can't outgive God. His generosity to us will always be greater than our generosity to Him. But His gracious gifts to us should prompt us to be grateful, and our giving is one way we show that gratitude. God gave His own son for us. We should delight in giving back to Him. So, decide what you can give and follow through. Don't give so other people will see you giving. Don't give because you're trying to bribe God into doing what you want. Give joyfully out of your gratitude for God's abundant grace. God loves a cheerful giver.

Give Cheerfully:

1. *Giving is not a way to gain status or influence.*

2. *Giving is not a way to purchase God's favor.*

3. *Giving should be a grateful response to what God has*

given to us.

THE TAKEAWAY: Give freely, joyfully, and abundantly. God loves a cheerful giver.

WEEKEND REFLECTION

"As for the rich in this present age, charge them not to be haughty, nor to set their hopes on the uncertainty of riches, but on God, who richly provides us with everything to enjoy" (1 Timothy 6:17).

FOR REFLECTION: You may not think of yourself as rich, but compared to the rest of the world, you are. Nearly half the world's population lives on less than $2.50 a day. If you have a roof over your head, running water in your bathroom, and know what you're having for breakfast tomorrow, in global terms you are rich. But don't put your hopes in your wealth. Put your hope on God. Thank God for giving you everything you need, and ask Him to increase your hope and trust in Him.

_____

_____

_____

_____

_____

_____

_____

_____

Week Fifty

MONDAY - For Such a Time

THE TEXT: *"And who knows whether you have not come to the kingdom for such a time as this?" (Esther 4:14).*

THE TALK: Esther was plucked from her home and taken into the king's harem. Life as a member of Xerxes' harem was not the life a good Jewish girl would have chosen. But God was with Esther. Her dignity and character helped her find favor with all she met, and Xerxes chose her to be his queen. But evil was lurking behind the scenes. Haman, one of the king's top advisers, had put plans in place to exterminate all the Jews in Persia. Mordecai, Esther's cousin, realized that God had brought her to this position so she could intervene and save her people.

When God elevates you, it is always for a purpose. Don't miss your moment. There may be risks. Esther risked her life to rescue her people. Without risks we don't need faith. If God has brought you this far, He will see you through. Step out in faith and trust Him.

It's Your Time:

1. *God always elevates you for a purpose.*

2. *Pay attention. You'll know the time when it comes.*

3. *Action requires risk. Take them in faith.*

THE TAKEAWAY: God has brought you here for a time such as this. Don't miss it.

TUESDAY – Are You Committed?

THE TEXT: *"But Ruth said, 'Do not urge me to leave you or to return from following you. For where you go I will go, and where you lodge I will lodge. Your people shall be my people, and your God my God'"* (Ruth 1:16).

THE TALK: Naomi, her husband, and her two sons traveled from Bethlehem to the land of Moab to escape a famine. Naomi's two sons married Moabite women, Orpah and Ruth. Then Naomi's husband and sons all died. Now a widow, Naomi decided to return home. She set out for Bethlehem with her two daughters-in-law accompanying her. But Naomi urged them to return home. She knew the deprivation and hardship that awaited them, and she could offer them no hope for a future. Oprah returned home, but Ruth stayed. Ruth irrevocably cast her lot with Naomi and Naomi's God. She was committed to following God and caring for Naomi whatever it took. Are we committed to following God, or do we just follow Him when it's convenient? The path of following Jesus is not always easy and smooth. Sometimes it requires us to leave our places of comfort and set out on a journey that we don't know how it will end. But if we don't go, we miss our blessing. Ruth found a home in Bethlehem, and God grafted the Moabite widow into Jesus' family tree. Where will your commitment take you?

True Commitment:

1. *Is willing to follow God even when it's costly.*

2. Is willing to follow God even when it's inconvenient.

3. Is willing to follow God in an uncertain present to reap a future blessing.

THE TAKEAWAY: Test your commitment to God, and don't turn back from following Him.

WEDNESDAY - New Beginnings

THE TEXT: *"And Joshua the son of Nun sent two men secretly from Shittim as spies, saying, 'Go, view the land, especially Jericho.' And they went and came into the house of a prostitute whose name was Rahab and lodged there"* (Joshua 2:1).

THE TALK: There is no sin in your past God won't redeem. Joshua sent spies to explore the land and gather information so he could form a battle plan. In Jericho the two men came to the house of Rahab, a prostitute. The king's men were on their trail, but Rahab hid the spies and sent the soldiers in the wrong direction. She told the two spies she knew Israel's God was the one true God and believed God had given them the land. She asked for mercy. The spies promised to protect her when they came to conquer the city and asked her to put a red cord in her window as a sign. When the wall around Jericho fell, only the portion where Rahab's home was remained standing. Rahab became part of the nation of Israel and married an Israelite man. The former Canaanite prostitute is one of five women named in Jesus' family tree. Don't think your past means God can't use you. Your past is there for God to redeem. Let Him rescue and restore you so you can find your destiny.

New Beginnings:

1. *God doesn't reject you because of your past.*

2. *Your past is an opportunity for God to redeem you.*

3. *God rescues you from your sin and restores you to your destiny.*

THE TAKEAWAY: When God offers redemption, He always offers a new beginning. Don't let your past keep you from finding your destiny.

THURSDAY - At the Crossroads

THE TEXT: "Thus says the Lord, 'Stand by the roads, and look, and ask for the ancient paths, where the good way is; and walk in it, and find rest for your souls'" (Jeremiah 6:16).

THE TALK: God doesn't leave us without direction. When you face a crossroads of decision, ask God which way to go and He will show you. God leads you in the ancient paths—paths laid out in the counsel of His Word and in accordance with His unchanging character. He leads you in ways that are good—meant to bless you and not do you harm. God promises that as we follow Him we will find rest for our souls. In moments of decision when you don't know which way to turn, ask God and follow His directions. He offers you rest.

When You're at the Crossroads:

1. *Look for the ancient paths already mapped out in God's Word.*

2. *Ask God to show you which way to go.*

3. *Follow the directions God gives you.*

THE TAKEAWAY: God's directions are meant to bless you and help you find rest for your soul. Follow Him.

FRIDAY - Spring is Come

THE TEXT: "*Behold, the winter is past; the rain is over and gone. The flowers appear on the earth, the time of singing has come*" (Song of Solomon 2:11-12).

THE TALK: Winter doesn't last forever. The winters in life are for a purpose. Sometimes there are things in our life that need to die so new life can bloom. Sometimes we just need to lie fallow, letting the rain of God's Spirit soak and soften our hearts so we're ready for planting season to come. But winter always turns to spring. Don't lose heart in the middle of your winter season. Flowers will bloom again. Spring will come. And when it does, rejoice! God will bring you a new season of life and restoration.

When Winter Seems Long:

1. *Remember that winters are in your life for a reason.*

2. *Winter won't last forever.*

3. *Get ready to rejoice! Spring will come.*

THE TAKEAWAY: No winter lasts forever. Get ready to celebrate. Your spring is on its way.

WEEKEND REFLECTION

"My heart and my flesh may fail, but God is the strength of my heart and my portion forever" (Psalm 73:26).

FOR REFLECTION: Our bodies may let us down. We may make mistakes. But God remains our strength and inheritance forever. When you fail, how does it encourage you to know God is your strength? What would be different about your life if you lived out of God's strength instead of your own? Ask God to help you rely on His strength this week.

DEVOTIONS FOR THE

Holidays

Holy Week

MONDAY - When They Don't Know

THE TEXT: "And Jesus said, 'Father, forgive them, for they know not what they do'" (Luke 23:34).

THE TALK: Roman soldiers crucified Jesus at Golgotha. They stripped Him naked and nailed Him to the cross, then sat down and cast lots for who would get His clothing. In the midst of His excruciating pain and suffering, Jesus prayed for His executioners, saying: *"Father, forgive them, for they know not what they do."* The soldiers didn't know the gravity of their crime; didn't recognize they were murdering the Lord of Life. Jesus offered them grace. Jesus offers you grace, too. There is no sin He hasn't seen, no time you've turned your back on Him that He's missed. He knows. He's seen it all, and He forgives you anyway. He took your place on the cross that you might live for Him. Every sin, every word spoken in anger, every act of willful disobedience—He paid for them all. Repent, and accept Jesus' forgiveness and grace.

Jesus' Forgiveness:

1. *Is offered freely.*

2. *Is offered completely.*

3. *Is offered redemptively.*

THE TAKEAWAY: Jesus offers you forgiveness. Will you accept it?

TUESDAY - It's Never Too Late

THE TEXT: *"And he said to him, 'Truly I say to you, today you will be with me in Paradise'"* (Luke 23:43).

THE TALK: Jesus' cross stood between the crosses of two criminals. As they hung there, one of the men railed at Him and mocked Him. But the other criminal rebuked the first and asked Jesus to remember Him. Jesus promised Him that He would be with Him in Paradise that very day. It's never too late to repent. You may think you're so far gone that Jesus can't rescue you, but until you breathe your last breath there is hope for forgiveness and redemption. Jesus welcomes all who turn to Him—whenever they turn to Him. So stop wasting time. Turn to Jesus and embrace your forgiveness.

Don't Wait:

1. *You're never too lost for Jesus to find you.*

2. *You're never too guilty for Jesus to forgive you.*

3. *You're never too unworthy for Jesus to give you grace.*

THE TAKEAWAY: Don't wait any longer. Ask Jesus to forgive you today.

WEDNESDAY - Never Forsaken

THE TEXT: *"And at the ninth hour Jesus cried with a loud voice, 'Eloi, Eloi, lema sabachthani?' which means, 'My God, my God, why have you forsaken me?'"* (Mark 15:34).

THE TALK: On the cross, Jesus' deepest cry of anguish came from the pain of His separation from God. Jesus bore our punishment on the cross, taking the full weight of humanity's sins upon himself. He experienced physical death, and He also experienced the spiritual death of being alienated from God. But despite His pain, Jesus was still confident of His resurrection. Jesus' cry from the cross echoes the first line of Psalm 22, a lament song that begins with anguish and ends with praise. God still turns our anguish into praise. You are not abandoned or forsaken. Jesus' death means that God will never turn His back on you again. Your suffering will not last forever. God will turn your pain into praise.

Not Rejected:

1. *Jesus' death means that we are no longer rejected.*

2. *Jesus' death means that we are no longer condemned.*

3. *Jesus' resurrection means we share His victory.*

THE TAKEAWAY: God has not rejected you. He will turn your pain into praise.

THURSDAY - It is Finished!

THE TEXT: *"When Jesus had received the sour wine, he said 'It is finished,' and he bowed His head and gave up His spirit"* (John 19:30).

THE TALK: Jesus' final breath was a victory cry—*telestai*, meaning "it is finished." Jesus had finished the mission the Father had given Him. The sacrifice was complete. Jesus had paid for the sins of the world with His own blood. Jesus' sacrifice is sufficient for you. There is nothing you need to do to add to what Jesus has already done for you. No good work, no offering, and no sacrifice on your behalf can make you any more forgiven than you are right now. The work of salvation is done. You don't have to earn it. Receive His grace.

It's Done:

1. *Jesus' death was a once-for-all sacrifice for all sin.*

2. *There's nothing you can do to make you any more*

forgiven than you already are.

3. *You don't have to earn God's grace. Just receive it.*

THE TAKEAWAY: Your sin, your past, or whatever it is in your life that keeps you from accepting salvation is finished. Accept His grace.

FRIDAY - Perfect Trust

THE TEXT: *"Then Jesus, calling out with a loud voice, said, 'Father, into your hands I commit my spirit!'"* (Luke 23:46).

THE TALK: After Jesus gave His victory cry, His final words were an expression of trust. Having completed His mission, Jesus committed His spirit to the Father. Imagine a child curling up in his father's lap to go to sleep. He knows he is safe in his daddy's embrace. As he surrendered to death, Jesus expressed that same kind of trust in His heavenly Father. We can trust God to care for us. Even when we walk through pain and suffering—even when obedience leads us to sacrifice— we can still trust our Father. Rest in your Father's arms. He won't let you down.

Trusting God:

1. *Trust God to care for you when life is hard.*

2. *Trust God to care for you in moments of surrender.*

3. *Trust that God will care for you when you need Him most.*

THE TAKEAWAY: Trust God like a child with his father. He cares for you.

WEEKEND REFLECTION

"He is not here, but has risen" (Luke 24:6).

FOR REFLECTION: Don't miss the wonder of that first Resurrection Sunday. The disciples expected to find Jesus in the tomb, but the grave was empty. Jesus was alive! He still lives. Don't look for Jesus in the grave. He is alive and He is with us, continuing to do a new thing in our world. Ask God to renew your wonder at the resurrection and to help you join Jesus where He is already at work.

_____

_____

_____

_____

_____

_____

_____

_____

_____

_____

_____

_____

_____

Christmas Week

MONDAY - Christmas Without Mary

THE TEXT: *"And the angel answered her, 'The Holy Spirit will come upon you, and the power of the Most High will overshadow you; therefore the child to be born will be called holy—the Son of God" (Luke 1:35).*

THE TALK: There would be no Christmas without Mary. The Bible doesn't tell us anything about her family, her personality, or her appearance. It only describes her as a virgin engaged to be married to Joseph, a man from the line of David. But it does give us one very important detail: she was willing. When Gabriel came to her with the astonishing news that she would be the mother of the Messiah, Mary could have said many things. But Mary received the word, accepted it, and obeyed. Are we also willing to be the bearers of the good news today? Are we willing to accept God's Word into our hearts and lives, let it grow within us, and share it with a waiting world?

Lessons from Mary:

1. *Mary received the word where she was.*

2. *Mary carried the word within her as it grew.*

3. *Mary delivered the word at the right moment when it was needed most.*

THE TAKEAWAY: God is still searching for someone to show favor to—someone who will receive, carry, and deliver His word. Will it be you?

❊

TUESDAY - Mary's Christmas

THE TEXT: *"And while they were there, the time came for her to give birth. And she gave birth to her firstborn son and laid him in a manger, because there was no place for them in the inn" (Luke 2:6-7).*

THE TALK: The conditions weren't ideal. Mary had a manger for a bassinet and a stable for a delivery room. There in a dark and dirty stable, Mary gave birth to the light of the world. Hope was born—God made flesh; the creator of the universe who now needed His diapers changed. It was humbling and holy, and Mary pondered the meaning of it all. Yet as the world tipped on its axis at the birth of a baby boy, the people of Bethlehem went about their business without realizing the world had forever changed. Are we guilty of doing something similar—celebrating Christmas and still missing the Savior? Where Mary pondered, we look for purchases. Where Mary sacrificed, we look for sales. And where Mary delivered God's Incarnate Word, we watch out the window for the delivery truck to come. Let's learn from Mary this Christmas. Slow down. Ponder. And make room for the Savior.

Learning from Mary:

1. Take time to celebrate Jesus' birth.

2. Consider what you will give to Jesus this year.

3. Meditate on the Christmas story and thank Jesus for coming.

THE TAKEAWAY: Stop, look, and remember what Christmas is all about: the Savior of the world.

WEDNESDAY - Cause and Effect

THE TEXT: *"And the angel said to them, 'Fear not, for behold, I bring you good news of great joy that will be for all the people. For unto you is born this day in the city of David a Savior, who is Christ the Lord'"* (Luke 2:10).

THE TALK: There is an often-overlooked cause and effect for Christmas. The cause is Jesus. The effect is joy. Jesus came to give us joy. Jesus' birth was the promise and hope of salvation. He was light in darkness, redemption for sin, hope for those perishing and afraid. Though the shepherds trembled when the sky filled with angels, they adjusted quickly. They went into Bethlehem to look for the child and glorified and praised God for what they had seen. If you want joy this Christmas, you need to find Jesus.

Finding Joy:

1. *Listen for the good news.*

2. *Look for the Savior.*

3. *Celebrate what God has done.*

THE TAKEAWAY: Put your eyes on Jesus and celebrate the joy of the season.

THURSDAY - Christmas List

THE TEXT: *"And going into the house they saw the child with Mary His mother, and they fell down and worshipped him. Then, opening their treasures, they offered him gifts, gold, and frankincense and myrrh"* (Matthew 2:11).

THE TALK: Christmas is a time for giving gifts. We make out our Christmas lists and take time to find the perfect gift for the people we love. But what do we give Jesus? The magi brought gifts that symbolized who Jesus was and the sacrifice

He would make on our behalf. Gold was an appropriate gift for the king of kings. Frankincense was a type of incense Jewish priests included with the meat during a burnt sacrifice. It represented Jesus as the high priest. And myrrh was used in burial, pointing to Jesus' sacrificial death. Jesus is still worthy of our gifts. What will you bring to Him?

Gifts for Jesus:

1. *Honor Jesus as the king of kings. Give Him your obedience.*

2. *Honor Jesus as the high priest. Give Him your worship.*

3. *Honor Jesus' sacrificial death for you. Give Him your heart.*

4. *Honor Jesus as your Lord. Give him your money.*

THE TAKEAWAY: The magi brought gifts to honor who Jesus was and what He will do. Give Him your gifts this Christmas.

FRIDAY - Seeing Our Salvation

THE TEXT: *"For my eyes have seen your salvation, that you have prepared in the presence of all peoples, a light for revelation to the Gentiles, and for glory to your people Israel"* (Luke 2:30-32).

THE TALK: When Mary and Joseph presented Jesus at the temple, Simeon was there. God had promised Simeon he would not die before he had seen the Messiah. When Jesus' parents brought Him into the temple Simeon recognized Jesus and he praised God, saying that now he had seen God's salvation. Simeon understood that Jesus had come to save all peoples—Gentiles and Jews alike. This Christmas, celebrate that Jesus brought salvation for the whole world. People who grow up in the church. People who have never darkened the door. People who look like us. People who don't. In Jesus, God gave salvation to us all, and we get the privilege of sharing the good news. Rejoice!

Rejoice:

1. *That we have seen Jesus, our salvation.*

2. *That Jesus brought salvation and grace for all peoples.*

3. *That we get the privilege of spreading the good news.*

THE TAKEAWAY: Christmas means that we get to see Jesus, the author of our salvation. Rejoice!

WEEKEND REFLECTION

"And suddenly there was with the angel a multitude of the heavenly host praising God and saying, 'Glory to God in the highest, and on earth peace among those with whom he is pleased!'" (Luke 2:13-14).

FOR REFLECTION: The angels rejoiced that Jesus had brought peace to those with whom God is pleased. God is pleased with us when we follow Jesus as Lord. How are you glorifying God this week? Thank God for sending Jesus, and ask Him to help you praise Him as you celebrate Christmas.

_____

_____

_____

_____

_____

_____

_____

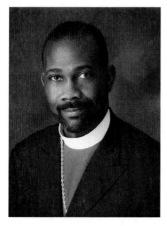

Bishop Geoffrey V. Dudley, Sr. is from Goldsboro, NC and is the youngest of 11 children from the union of the late Bishop Leamon Dudley, Sr. the late Mrs. Ida Dorothy Dudley. He gave his life to Christ when he was 12 years old and began ministry at the early age of 13. Bishop Dudley is married to the former Glenda D. Jones of Spring Hope, NC. They have two children, Mahogany Kneecoal and Geoffrey Vincient II. He is a retired Air Force Chaplain Lieutenant Colonel, and in his 21 ½ years of service he has lived and ministered in many states and several countries. He diligently pursued formal education to prepare for a lifetime of ministry.

- **1981** – Bachelor of Arts, Communication, Drama
  & Speech, University of North Carolina at Greensboro

- **1991** – Master of Divinity, School of Theology,
  Virginia Union University

- **1992** – Master of Human Relations, University of
  Oklahoma

- **1997** – Post Master Education Specialist,
  University of Memphis

- **2000** – Doctor of Ministry, Samuel Dewitt Proctor
  School of Theology, Virginia Union University

- **2015**-Present – Pursuing PhD in Organizational
  Leadership from Regents University

Bishop Dudley has Episcopal responsibility over several churches/ministries and coaches several pastors/leaders through Changing Lives Ministries. He has dedicated his life to serving the church and community through a variety of organizations. Bishop Dudley is the founding pastor of one of the fastest growing churches in the Metro East (O'Fallon, IL) area of St. Louis, MO. LifeChangers, as they call themselves, are committed to changing lives in their lifetime.